A HANDBOOK FOR TEACHERS IN UNIVERSITIES AND COLLEGES

A HANDBOOK FOR TEACHERS IN UNIVERSITIES & COLLEGES

A GUIDE TO IMPROVING TEACHING METHODS

c 1989

DAVID NEWBLE & ROBERT CANNON

ILLUSTRATIONS BY ZIG KAPELIS

St. Martin's Press
New York

First published in the United States of America in 1989

Printed in Great Britain

ISBN 0-312-03196-3 paperback

Library of Congress Cataloging-in-Publication Data
Newble, David.
A handbook for teachers in universities and colleges: a guide to improving teaching methods/David Newble and Robert Cannon: illustrations by Zig Kapelis.
p.c.m.
Includes bibliographies and index.
ISBN 0-312-03198-3 : $15.95 (est.)
1. College teaching. I. Cannon, Robert (Robert Anthony)
II. Title
LB2331.N43 1989 89-6044
378'.125--dc19 CIP

Typeset by DP Photosetting, Aylesbury, Bucks
Printed in Great Britain by
Martin's of Berwick, Berwick on Tweed

Contents

Foreword

An increasing number of universities and colleges around the world are, belatedly, realizing that they have a responsiblity for the initial training and in-service training of their academic staff. This realization has come in various ways. In some places it has been through pressure from students who have complained about the standard of teaching. Elsewhere the staff themselves have put pressure on their administrative colleagues to provide resources for preparing them for their teaching function more adequately. But perhaps the most insistent pressure, and one which is gathering momentum in several countries, is the demand by government for staff appraisal to demonstrate that universities and colleges are being fully efficient in their use of resources.

Whatever the source of the pressure, it is particularly timely for *A Handbook for Teachers in Universities and Colleges* to be published. This book has been adapted from a previous Handbook designed for clinical teachers. That Handbook was so popular that the authors have been persuaded to develop their ideas and format for a broader range of their colleagues. I was one of those who found their previous book refreshingly different from what was then available. It managed to combine basic practical advice with a firm rationale, and yet that advice was presented in a readable manner and leavened with humour. Too often books providing advice for university and college teachers have a weak rationale, relying solely on anecdote and 'gut feelings' about teaching, or they draw on dubiously relevant research findings and then become dogmatic about procedures which in reality should always take into account the important differences in style in the way people prefer to teach. I was delighted to find that the present book has the qualities of its predecessor and has also been brought up to date by drawing on some of the most recent ideas on teaching and learning in higher education.

Clearly this Handbook could be used to support the training programmes being introduced into colleges and universities around the world. The various chapters focus on the specific skills which are dealt with in such programmes – large group and small group teaching, methods of assessment and so on. The information is sufficiently detailed to provide help for the beginning lecturer and interesting suggestions for those with more experience.

There is a particular need to try new ways of organizing and presenting lecture material when there is less mobility in the profession, otherwise staleless creeps into the teaching and students soon react to the lack of enthusiasm. It is also crucial to keep challenging traditional ways of teaching in the light of modern technological developments: are there better ways of presenting information these days? The lecture method had its origins in the time before printing when students in the medieval universities were required to attend the reading of the inaccessible handwritten books. We now have not only books, but a wide range of audiovisual and computer-based methods for presenting information, and yet lectures are still the most widely used way of transfering ideas to students. Is their continued use based on their proved effectiveness, or is it derived from a lack of knowledge of the alternatives, or a resistance to change? Whatever the reasons, this Handbook will offer a range of alternatives to the lecture, as well as indicating ways of making lecturing itself more effective.

Although this book is organized in a way which takes the lecturer through the various teaching techniques, there is another way to read it. One way of improving the effectiveness of higher education is to train teachers to be more effective in their use of the various specific techniques, but this method cannot provide a fully effective rationale for deciding how to 'orchestrate' the various techniques. An alternative approach, and one which I favour, is to focus instead on the quality of student learning. How do we develop an institutional environment that most effectively promotes learning? Of course, this will depend in part on having effective teachers, but it will also depend on the learning resources available, on the philosophy underlying the curriculum, on choice of topics within the syllabus, on the type of assignments students are required to do and the choice given among them, on the feedback they are given on that work, and on the assessment procedures which govern what type of learning and knowledge is rewarded. For anyone wanting to follow that alternative strategy in thinking about how to improve departmental teaching and learning, this Handbook could be read in a different order. Start with the final chapter on student learning. Consider the meaning of a *deep approach* to learning. Look at the suggestions which follow on how to facilitate that deep approach, and then use those ideas to provide a rationale within which to decide, as you read the other chapters, why you would use one or other of the techniques described and how you would orchestrate them into an effective environment to support high quality of learning. It is, after all, learning which is the end product of the education system and not the 'production methods' of teaching.

That alternative approach is, of course, just a personal preference, and as most of my research effort has been directed towards understanding how students go about learning and studying, that recommendation has to be judged in that light. The authors provide valuable suggestions for additional reading, among which *The Experience of Learning* spells out the justification for concentrating more on the quality of student learning. To their list might be added a very recent publication which relates research on student learning to the practice of teaching – *Improving Learning*, edited by Paul Ramsden and published by Kogan Page in 1988.

All in all, this Handbook provides a welcome addition to the books available for supporting teachers in tertiary education. It provides detailed information about both traditional and innovatory techniques, it contains many valuable tips to make teaching both more enjoyable and more effective, it is sure to stimulate thinking about teaching and learning, and above all it is enjoyable to read.

NOEL ENTWISTLE
Bell Professor of Education
University of Edinburgh

Preface

In 1983 we published a book entitled *A Handbook for Clinical Teachers*. We did so for two reasons. Firstly, because we recognized that medical students were being taught to a large extent by people who had undertaken little or no formal study in the field of education. Secondly, because few books had been written to aid the teacher wishing to gain a perspective on basic educational principles and how these might be applied to teaching. The Handbook received a very positive response and after several reprints a second edition was published in 1987.

Rather surprisingly, we found that the book was being read by teachers outside the medical faculty who told us that the same problems existed for them and that the medical examples and orientation did not prevent them using the information, materials and advice in their own field. However, we were aware that a book specifically on medical teaching must inevitably have limitations. We have, therefore, modified the book to suit a wider audience. In some cases this has involved straightforward editing. In other cases, certain sections and indeed whole chapters have been completely rewritten. Inevitably, when writing for a wide audience there is a problem of selecting helpful examples of teaching or learning concerns: what will appeal to a teacher of literature may not appeal to a teacher of engineering. We have therefore striven to select from different disciplines in our choice of examples but where we felt the medical examples from our earlier book were helpful and relevant they have been retained. We trust that readers from other disciplines will be able to interpret these examples for their own needs. In making these modifications, we hope we have retained the character which has been so successful in the earlier versions of the Handbook. We look forward to receiving as much feedback about this book as we did from the medical version.

Finally we would like to express appreciation to our secretarial staff, in particular Ermioni Mourtzios; to MTP Press, the publishers of the medical version of the Handbook; and to

Kogan Page, particularly our editor Dolores Black, for their support of this new project.

DAVID NEWBLE
ROBERT CANNON
Adelaide, 1989

Chapter 1 Teaching in Large Groups

INTRODUCTION

Large group teaching is dominated by the lecture method. However, there are important and educationally useful techniques that can be used to improve the quality of lectures. There are also variations of the lecture method that can be introduced to encourage more active participation of students.

This chapter assumes that you have been asked to give a lecture or series of lectures and that you are keen to enhance the chances of the students learning and remembering what you have taught. To do this you will need a basic understanding of the factors which are likely to influence the learning of the students during the lecture, as well as a range of suitable techniques.

STUDENT LEARNING

Educational research allows us to make a few broad generalizations about student learning in a lecture. On the basis of such research, Bligh argues persuasively that the lecture is as effective as most other methods of transmitting information but is less effective than other methods for encouraging thought or changing attitudes. However, it is still possible to promote thinking and to change attitudes in the lecture by using techniques discussed later in this chapter.

Important considerations in learning are memory, arousal, motivation, structure and feedback. **Memory** has two components – short-term and long-term. In essence, your task is to get accurate information into short-term memory and aid its rapid transfer into long-term memory. Only a limited amount of information can be retained in the short-term memory and its decay is very rapid. It is vulnerable to many outside influences, some of which can be minimized by the lecturer. Information will not be transferred to long-term memory unless it is understood. This cannot be achieved unless the student is attending to what you are saying. Attention will be determined by the students' level of arousal and degree of motivation. **Arousal** implies a general state of readiness of the brain to accept new information and **motivation** implies a willingness to direct brain activity to a specific task. Above all else, the teacher's role is to increase the level of arousal and to maintain it. What happens, hypothetically, to a student's level of performance during a traditional uninterrupted lecture is graphically displayed by the heavy line in Figure 1.1. It shows a rapid and continuous decline after the first few minutes, with the slight renewal of interest just before the end. The graph also indicates the potential value of a rest period which increases attention and results in a learning gain outweighing the amount of learning lost during the rest period. Interestingly, a graph of lecturer performance would closely parallel that of student performance.

FIGURE 1.1

HYPOTHESIZED PATTERN OF STUDENT LEVEL OF PERFORMANCE SHOWING A PROGRESSIVE FALL IN ATTENTION AND LEARNING DURING AN UNINTERRUPTED LECTURE AND CONTRASTING THIS WITH THE GAIN OBTAINED FROM INTRODUCING A REST PERIOD (AFTER BLIGH, 1971)

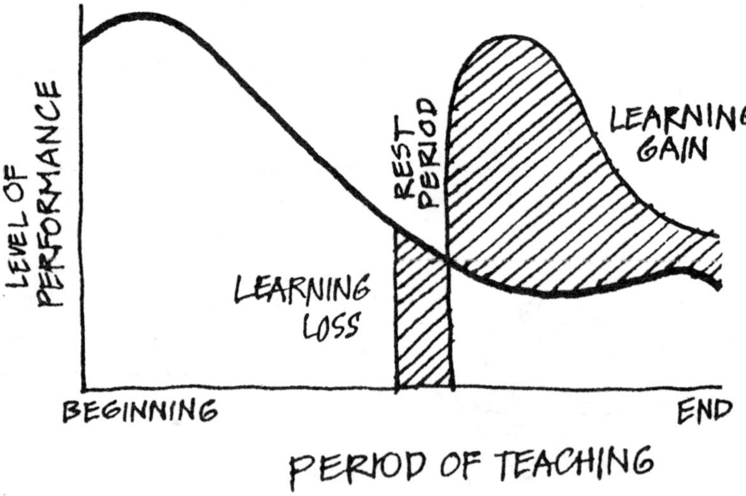

Motivation is such a key factor that it appears to be more important in learning than intelligence. The problem is that students are motivated by different things. Common motivators are the relevance of the material to ultimate careers, the generation of a feeling of curiosity early in the lecture, the enthusiasm of the teacher for the subject, positive feedback and, not surprisingly, examinations.

Having attained the required degree of arousal and motivation you will still not succeed unless you use techniques which aid the student's understanding of the material to be presented. The lecture must be organized into a **logical structure** which is comprehended by the class. It is appropriate to describe this structure at the beginning of the lecture or present it in a visual form (blackboard, overhead transparency, handout). You should also be aware that memory will be further enhanced by giving relevant examples of the points made, by explaining new concepts in terms of familiar ones (ie using analogies), and by incorporating opportunities for the students to review and use the information already covered. Specific techniques of doing so are described later.

Feedback, particularly positive feedback in which reward is more prominent than punishment, facilitates learning. One study showed that students tested on the subject material at the end of a lecture retained more over the next few weeks than did those not tested.

Effectiveness of learning is also enhanced if your lecture supports and builds on previous information. This highlights the need for the lecturer to avoid making assumptions about knowledge obtained from previous lectures and courses.

THE PURPOSE OF THE LECTURE

As a rule, lecturers attempt to achieve too much in their lectures. This problem is aggravated if the task is to give a single lecture on a specific topic rather than a series of lectures to cover a wider area. In general terms, you should decide whether the main purpose of the lecture is to motivate the students so that they appreciate the importance of the subject material, whether it is to transmit a body of information not readily available elsewhere, or whether it is to have the student leave the lecture having learned some important concepts and principles. True, you may be forced to try and achieve all of these in a single lecture. If so, it should be structured to deal with them sequentially not concurrently. If you are lucky enough to have a series of lectures to give then the problems are not so great.

THE CONTEXT OF THE LECTURE

Your lecture has a place in the curriculum and hopefully a carefully planned place. All too frequently, however, the only information you will receive from curriculum planners will be the title of the lecture. As a minimum, you will then need to obtain a copy of the relevant part of the curriculum to see how your topic fits in. You might try contacting the curriculum committee or head of the department for specific details of what they wish you to teach. Do not be surprised if you are told that you are the expert and should know what the students should be taught! You may also try talking to the lecturers preceding you, particularly those whom you might assume will teach some facts or principles on which you intend to rely. In general it is unwise to assume that the students have learned (even if they have been taught) anything that is vital to their understanding of your lecture. It is only after a realistic appraisal of the context of your contribution that you can rationally set about its planning.

WHAT DO THE STUDENTS REQUIRE OF THE LECTURER?

Several studies have attempted to define what students think are the characteristics of a good lecturer. One such list includes 43 components, the most frequently quoted of which are seen in Figure 1.2. It is well worth critically evaluating your lecture performance against these criteria.

FIGURE 1.2
SOME ATTRIBUTES OF THE GOOD LECTURER (AFTER COOPER AND FOY, 1967)

- Presents the material clearly and logically.
- Enables the student to understand the basic principles of the subject.
- Can be heard clearly.
- Makes the material intelligibly meaningful.
- Adequately covers the ground.
- Maintains continuity in the course.
- Is constructive and helpful in his/her criticism.

- Shows an expert knowledge of the subject.
- Adopts an appropriate pace during the lecture.
- Includes material not readily accessible in textbooks.
- Is concise.
- Illustrates the practical applications of the theory of the subject.

PREPARING THE LECTURE

Define the purpose

Having clarified the context of the lecture to the best of your ability the time has come to get down to some detailed planning. The best way to start is to write down the purpose(s) of the lecture. We say write down advisedly because nothing clarifies the mind more than putting pen to paper!

Identify the content

Now set about identifying the content. We suggest you start by initially jotting down the main ideas, theories and examples

FIGURE 1.3 METHOD OF IDENTIFYING THE CONTENT FOR A LECTURE (AFTER BUZAN, 1974)

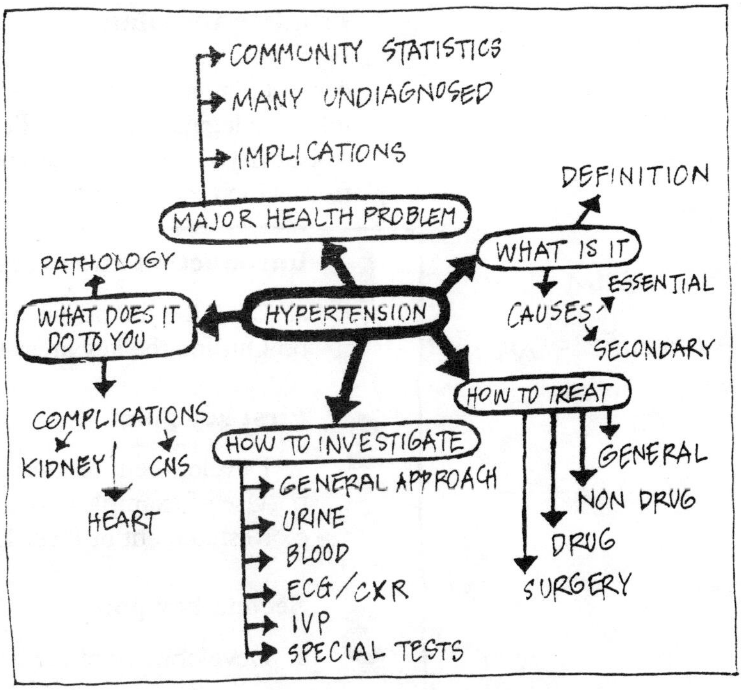

that come to mind around the central purpose of the lecture. This should be done during a period of free thinking without any particular concern for the order in which you may eventually wish to present the ideas in the lecture. Figure 1.3 illustrates a way of doing this which has been found to be helpful by staff attending our courses for new lecturers.

The lecture topic (in this case, taken from a medical lecture on hypertension) is placed in the centre of the paper and the main points to be made are written down as indicated. When the main ideas are identified, further points will tend to branch out as you think more carefully about them. This process is continued until you have exhausted all your ideas. You may at this stage find that you need to read around some of the ideas in order to refine them or to bring yourself up to date.

During this exercise you will find that illustrative examples of key points come to mind. Jot these down also. In addition you should be on the look out for illustrations from which you might prepare slides or other audiovisual aids. Appropriate jokes or cartoons may be collected during this exercise.

Finalize the plan

Now you must finalize the plan of the lecture. The rough content plan must be transformed into a linear structure which follows a logical sequence. There is no single best way of doing so but if you are a novice you may prefer a formal structure from which to work. One such structure is seen in Figure 1.4.

FIGURE 1.4

A LECTURE PLAN

1 **Introduction and overview**

a. Describe the purpose of the lecture.
b. Outline the key areas to be covered.

2 **First key point**

a. Development of ideas.
b. Use of examples.
c. Restatement of **first key point.**

3 **Second key point**

a. Development of ideas.

b. Use of examples.
c. Restatement of **first and second points.**

4 Third key point

a. Development of ideas.
b. Use of examples.
c. Restatement of **first, second and third points**.

5 Summary and conclusion

Part of such a plan that was developed for the lecture on hypertension outlined previously is shown in Figure 1.5. The plan also includes notations for the inclusion of visual material, such as overhead transparencies and slides.

FIGURE 1.5

PART OF A DETAILED LECTURE PLAN

TITLE : HYPERTENSION

1 INTRODUCTION
FIVE KEY POINTS TO BE COVERED (OVERHEAD)
A. THE NATURE AND EXTENT OF THE PROBLEM
B. WHAT IS HYPERTENSION AND ITS CAUSES
C. WHAT DOES IT DO TO YOU
D. INVESTIGATION
E. TREATMENT

2 THE PROBLEM
A. DBP > 90 LEADS TO SIGNIFICANT MORBIDITY/MORTALITY (SLIDE - ACTUAL STATISTICS)
B. 10-25% ADULT POPULATION HAS HYPERTENSION BUT OFTEN UNDIAGNOSED OR INEFFECTIVELY TREATED
C. TREATMENT REDUCES MORBIDITY/MORTALITY (SLIDE - VETERAN'S STUDY FROM USA)
D. IMPLICATIONS OF SCREENING - DIAGNOSIS, COST, EDUCATION

3 WHAT IS HYPERTENSION
A. MULTIFACTORIAL (SLIDE - VARIOUS FACTORS)
B. ESSENTIAL AND SECONDARY
C. CAUSES OF SECONDARY HYPERTENSION (SLIDE)

This is the classical content-oriented lecture plan. You may wish to be more ambitious and use a **problem-centred plan**.

This requires extra thought but done well is likely to be rewarding. It is a technique suited to the lecture in which the primary purpose is to get students to learn major concepts and principles rather than to transmit factual information. In this case the lecturer opens with the statement of the problem, often presented in the form of a real-life situation. Students are led through a consideration of a variety of possible solutions. The method is ideal for encouraging student participation during the lecture.

PRESENTING THE LECTURE

Having decided what you intend to teach, you must now give careful attention to how you are going to present it to the students. Let us assume that it is to be your first contact with this group of students. Your recently acquired knowledge of educational research tells you that before any learning can take place the students must be aroused and you must structure your lecture so that this arousal level is maintained. You may wish to obtain their attention initially by devising an arresting opening to the lecture. Ways of doing this are limited only by your personality and your imagination. A joke, a movie clip, an anecdote, a quotation or a discussion with a few of the audience may generate interest. However, it must be borne in mind that the attention of the students ought to be engaged by the subject of the lecture rather than the personality of the lecturer. The danger of the latter has become known as the 'Dr Fox effect' based on an experiment where an actor (Dr Fox) gave a lecture comprising meaningless double-talk which fooled experienced listeners into believing that they had participated in a worthwhile and stimulating learning experience.

Starting the lecture

Particular attention needs to be given to the way you start your lecture. For many teachers, this is the most difficult aspect of teaching. It is essential to decide beforehand exactly how you intend to start. Do not leave this decision until you are facing the students.

Perhaps the easiest way to start is to explain the purpose of the lecture and how it is organized. An outline on the blackboard showing your lecture plan is a good way of doing this. Such visual material will take attention away from yourself, give you something to talk to and allow you to settle down. Writing the plan on the board gives students a permanent reminder of the structure of your lecture.

Once you become more confident, other issues should be considered. You must become sensitive to the students' degree of arousal and their motivation to learn your material. It is often helpful to arrive early and chat with some of the students before the lecture to establish their level of previous knowledge. Alternatively, you can start by asking a few pertinent questions, taking care that this is done in a non-threatening manner. Should you establish that serious deficiencies in knowledge are present you must be flexible enough to try and correct them rather than plough on regardless into your prepared lecture.

Varying the format

You should now give attention to the body of the lecture. Student attention must be considered. A purely verbal presentation will not be very effective and will contribute to a fall off in the level of arousal. You should therefore be planning ways of incorporating some of the techniques described in the next section. Research studies have shown us that levels of arousal and learning will fall progressively. No more than 20 minutes should go by before the students are given a break or before the teaching technique is significantly altered. Ways of doing this include questioning or testing the students, generating discussion among students and using an audiovisual aid. These are discussed in more detail later.

Finishing the lecture

The conclusion of the lecture is as important as the introduction. Your closing comments should also be well prepared. The last things that you say are the ones the students are most likely to remember. This will be the opportunity to reiterate the key points you hope to have made. You may also wish to direct students to additional reading at this time, but be reasonable in your expectations and give them a clear indication of what is essential as opposed to what you think is desirable. A couple of minutes to allow them to consolidate and read their notes is a worthwhile technique.

Rehearsal

Some of the best lecturers find it very helpful to rehearse so a dry run may be even more important for the less experienced. However, the purpose of the rehearsal should not be to become word perfect. You must retain the flexibility to allow yourself to digress should the necessity occur. A rehearsal will often reveal that you are attempting to cram too much into the time and that some of your visual aids are poorly prepared or difficult to see from the rear of the theatre. The value of a rehearsal will be much enhanced if you invite along a colleague to act as the audience and to provide critical comments.

In some institutions you will have access to courses on teaching methods. Overcome your natural reticence and enrol. It is likely that one component of the course will give you the opportunity of viewing your lecturing technique on videotape. The unit running the course may also provide an individual to come and observe your lecture, giving you the expert feedback you may not always get from a colleague.

Rehearsal may also give you the confidence to leave behind the full text of the lecture. (If you have the full text with you, you will be tempted to read it and thus ensure a rapid decline in levels of arousal.) Many good lecturers only bring with them a list of key points, often written on small pocket-sized cards numbered in serial order. Others rely on slides and overhead transparencies to guide them.

WHAT ADDITIONAL TECHNIQUES ARE AVAILABLE?

We have already stressed how variety in the presentation is essential in maintaining arousal. Ways of doing this may be categorized into variations in the manner and style of presentation, active participation of the students and use of audio-visual aids.

Variations in manner and style

It is important that you feel comfortable with the way you present your lecture. However, you should not necessarily limit your manner and style to that of your basic personality. Changes in the volume and rate of speech, the use of silence, the maintenance of eye contact with the class and movement away from the lectern to create a less formal relationship should all be considered.

Active participation

A powerful way of enhancing learning is to devise situations which require the students to interact with you and with each other. **Questions** are the simplest form of interaction. Many lecturers ask for questions at the end of their presentation but most are disappointed in the student response. Others direct questions at students during the lecture and this may be effective in producing a high level of arousal. However, unless the lecturer is very careful, the dominant emotion may be one of fear. It is therefore preferable to create a situation in which all students answer the questions. You may wish to prepare a question in the form of a multiple-choice item which can be projected as a slide or an overhead transparency. Understanding can be checked by asking for a show of hands for each alternative answer to the question. You should follow-up by explaining why each alternative is or is not a suitable answer.

The Socratic method, when thoughtfully used in a non-threatening manner, may be a stimulating approach. This method builds understanding by a carefully prepared sequence of questions and student answers.

If you wish to develop your questioning technique further we suggest you refer to the books written by Brown and by Cannon.

Small group activity within a large group should always be considered as a variation as it is a powerful teaching technique. Surprisingly, it is uncommonly attempted in the lecture even though it is simple to arrange for a large number of students in a theatre of any size. Once you try it out you may find it so exciting to hear the steady hum of students actually discussing your subject that you will never again feel comfortable giving a didactic lecture. The general approach is to break down the class into small groups, using a judicious rearrangement of seating if necessary. Small groups of two to four people may be formed among neighbours without any movement while larger groups may be quickly formed by two to four students in one row turning to form a group with students in the row behind. If a substantial amount of discussion time is planned the groups might best be formed at the beginning of the lecture and asked to spread themselves out to use up the whole lecture theatre space. The selection of the most appropriate grouping will largely depend on what you wish to achieve. Small groups may be asked to discuss a limited topic for a few minutes (sometimes called buzz groups) or to consider broader topics for a longer period of time. You may then wish to allow all or some of the groups to report back to you. This is a very useful exercise when problems are given to the students to solve and where a variety of different responses can be expected. Some more specific examples of small group activity are now discussed.

One-to-one discussion is a particularly valuable technique in the situation where you might wish all the class to consider a very emotive or challenging concept. This method is described in detail in the chapter on small group teaching.

Reading or problem-solving activities may be introduced. These can involve a combination of individual study and small group discussion. There are many variations on this strategy and one example is described here.

Students are instructed to bring their text to lectures or a handout is provided consisting, perhaps, of an article, a summary, a quotation, a set of diagrams or equations. A directed-reading, or problem-solving, task is set. This task should involve the students for 5–10 minutes. At the end of this period of individual work students are instructed to discuss something with the person beside them. They may, for instance, be asked to compare answers, draw conclusions, raise issues, identify misunderstandings or make evaluative judgements. The students are then asked for feedback. Depending on the size of the group you could ask for reports from all or some of the pairs, have pairs report to another pair and seek general reports from these larger groups, or have a show of hands to questions or issues you have identified as you moved around the class during the discussion phase. Alternatively you could ask students to write on cards, then collect these, and collate the information after the lecture as a basis for your teaching in the next lecture. Conclude by drawing ideas together, summing-up, or whatever is appropriate to the task you set them.

Whatever you do – and this is critical – thoroughly plan the activity: clearly structure the time and the tasks set, and stick to your plan (unless there are *very* good reasons to change). Your instructions, including the time available and tasks to be carried out, should be clearly displayed on a handout, or on the board, for ready reference during the exercise.

Brainstorming is a technique which can be modified for use in the lecture situation. It can be of value at the beginning of a lecture to stimulate interest in the topic to be discussed. The students are presented with an issue or a problem and asked to contribute as many ideas or solutions as they can. All contributions are accepted without comment or judgement as to their merits and written on the blackboard or on an overhead transparency. This approach encourages 'lateral' or 'divergent' thinking. One of us has successfully used this technique with a class of 120 at the beginning of a lecture. The session commenced with a request for the class to put forward their suggestions in response to a question. These suggestions were then categorized and used as a basis for further discussion by the lecturer in an environment where the students had been the initiators of the discussion points. Brainstorming is discussed further in Chapter 3 on small group teaching.

Use of audiovisual aids

The technical aspects of preparing and using audiovisual aids are discussed in detail in Chapter 7. This section will discuss their use in the lecture for a variety of purposes including illustrating the structure, providing examples, stimulating interest and providing variety. The aids most likely to be used are the blackboard (see page 132), overhead transparencies, slides, films or videotapes and demonstrations.

The overhead projector is now widely used in teaching. It has the advantages of allowing the lecturer to prepare material beforehand and to retain the information for future use. It also avoids the need to turn one's back to the audience. An overhead transparency is particularly useful for giving outlines and listing key points. A blank sheet of paper can be used to reveal the points in sequence. A pen or pencil placed on the transparency itself should be used to direct the students' attention to the appropriate point rather than using the pointer on the screen. Information may be added to the transparency as the lecture proceeds.

We have found that the value of the overhead is seriously reduced by four common practices. First, too much information is included on each transparency. Secondly, the lecturer works through the material too quickly or talks about something different while students are trying to read and take notes from the screen. Thirdly, the transparency is carelessly positioned or out of focus. Fourthly, and the most common abuse, is that material on transparencies is far too small to be read by students.

The 35 mm slide is widely used and some lecturers build up an extensive collection. These too are often misused. In general, slides containing verbal material should be kept simple and must be clearly visible at the back of the theatre. Care must be taken when reproducing material from books and journals which often contain far too much information. Do not be guilty of introducing your slide with words such as 'This is a complex slide but I just want you to concentrate on this line of figures'. Coloured slides of relevant material and examples are ideal for illustrating didactic points and for adding variety and interest.

When using slides, avoid turning off the lights for more than brief periods. The level of arousal will rapidly fall, however interesting your slides happen to be.

Films and videotapes are best used in short segments. Their use requires more careful planning as it will be necessary to have a projectionist if a film is to be shown and probably a technician to set up video equipment. However, the effort is well worthwhile for both the impact of the content and the variety it introduces in the lecture. We use such material to show illustrative examples and practical techniques. Films or videotapes may also be used in attempts to influence attitudes or to explore emotionally charged areas in the lecture setting.

A short segment can be shown illustrating some challenging situation (trigger film) and the class asked to react to this situation. Films for this purpose are commercially available in some disciplines.

Some lecturers choose to show a full-length film or video in the lecture hour. The educational value of this is questionable unless the material is carefully integrated into the teaching. This integration can be done by:

- very carefully selecting and previewing the film;
- during the preview, preparing notes on how you intend to link the film to the course, how you will introduce it, what activity the students might engage in during or after viewing it, and how you will conclude the film session;
- using the film in the way you plan and ensuring you have ample time for all the viewing and related activities.

If you believe that a film is particularly important you can enhance its value by showing it twice: first to introduce students to it; second to focus attention (through the use of prepared questions or tasks) on specific matters of importance.

Demonstrating

There are several ways in which demonstration can be used as an integral part of a lecture. Some lecturers regard their lectures as 'demonstrations-of-the-scholar-at-work'. Another way of putting this is to say that they **profess** their discipline in the lecture. This style of lecturing is typified by demonstrations of reasoning about something, problem-solving, developing an idea or criticizing a text. This approach can often be very confusing to students and needs to be used with very great care indeed. We sometimes think it is used as a way of excusing scant attention to lecture preparation, if the actual delivery of this approach is a reliable guide!

Quite another form of demonstration is the **procedural demonstration.** As this may often involve materials and equipment of some kind it is essential that all students can see the demonstration clearly. This is often quite impossible in large lecture theatres. You could deal with this problem by using video, either by mounting a camera above the demonstration to display pictures to monitors in the theatre or by using prepared videotapes (see pages 136–42 for assistance with this).

However, there is a danger that the demonstration may become another source of boredom. If possible it should be made into an active learning occasion. One strategy of doing so is to direct students to make specific observations during the demonstration against a number of specified criteria or, even better, to have them generate their own criteria (which can be a very important intellectual task in its own right). Another strategy is to use the demonstration as a source of data to replace the reading or problem-solving activities used in the technique described on pages 12–13.

Handouts

Some research has been done on the use of handouts and this suggests that students get higher test scores from lectures accompanied by handouts, that students appreciate them, and that the design of the handout influences note-taking practices. One study showed that students preferred to write in the space between headings and the more space left, the more notes were taken.

Handouts may be valuable as a guide to the structure of the lecture and in this case may be very similar in content to the basic lecture plan. Such a handout should be given out at the beginning of a lecture. You may wish to use the handout to provide detailed information on an area not well covered in standard student texts or not covered in detail during the lecture. Such handouts should be given out at the end of the lecture. Handouts may also be used to guide further study and to provide references for additional reading. Whenever you distribute handouts, it is essential that you use them in some way during the lecture to reduce the probability that they will be filed and forgotten or used as paper aeroplanes!

Student note-taking

The research in this area generally supports the view that note-taking should be encouraged. It is a process which requires the student to attend to the lecture. The process of encoding the information into notes is one which aids its transfer into long-term memory, particularly if students can be persuaded to read their notes shortly after the lecture is completed. The lecturer can assist this process by providing a structure for material that is complex. Diagrams and other schematic representations may be more valuable than simple prose.

WHEN THINGS GO WRONG

Throughout this book we present the view that things are less likely to go wrong if you have carefully prepared yourself for the task. However, unexpected problems can and do arise, so strategies to deal with these need to be part of your teaching skills.

In our experience problems are likely to fall into one of the following categories.

Problems with audio-visual materials and equipment

An equipment failure can be a potential disaster if you have prepared a series of slides or transparencies for projection. Preventive measures include having back-up equipment on hand and learning to change blown bulbs or remove jammed slides. If these measures are of no avail, you will have to continue on without the materials and may do so successfully provided that you have taken care to have a clear record in your notes of the content of your slides or transparencies. Photocopied enlargements of slides of data are a useful back-up here. You may then be able to present some of the information verbally, on a blackboard or whiteboard, or on an overhead transparency if the original problem was with the slide projector. You will not, of course, be able to use this approach with illustrations and you may have to substitute careful description and perhaps blackboard sketches to cover essential material. Whatever you do, do not pass around your materials, which may be damaged and, of course, by the time most of the audience receive them, they are no longer directly relevant to what you are saying.

Problems with your presentation

Losing your place and running out of time can be disconcerting. Do not start apologizing or communicate your sense of 'panic' if these should happen. Instead, pause, calmly evaluate your situation, decide on a course of action and continue.

Problems with students

Lecturers often fear confrontation with students in a lecture class. We cannot go into all aspects of classroom management and discipline here, but we can identify a number of principles and refer you to more detailed discussions elsewhere (McKeachie's *Teaching Tips* is a useful reference).

Disruptive behaviour and talking in class are common problems and must not be ignored, both for the sake of your own concentration and for the majority of students who are there to hear what you have to say. Minor disturbances can usually be overcome by simply stopping talking and waiting patiently for quiet. If this happens more than once the other students will usually make their displeasure known to the offenders. If the disruption is more serious, you will have to speak directly to the students concerned and make them understand that you are aware of the offence. But do try initially to treat it with humour or you may alienate the rest of the class. If the problem persists, indicate that you will be unable to tolerate the situation again and that you will have to ask them to leave. Make sure you do just this if the problem re-emerges. Do so firmly and calmly. If the situation leads to confrontation, it is probably best if you leave the room. It is remarkable what effect this has on disciplining a group of students! Make every attempt to meet the offenders afterwards to deal with the problem.

We have been appalled at accounts of lecturers who endure the most unreasonable physical and verbal abuse in lectures and do nothing about it – other than suffer inwardly. There is no need for this and the majority of students will respect firm but fair disciplinary measures. An added measure is to arrange arriving and leaving lectures so that you have time to get to know at least some of the students in the class – especially potentially troublesome ones.

EVALUATING THE LECTURE

Improving the quality of your lecturing will depend on a combination of experience and your willingness to critically evaluate your performance. Evaluation may be seen as *informal* or *formal*. The informal way may involve asking several students whom you know for their comments. It may also be undertaken by asking yourself a series of questions immediately after the lecture:

- How much time was taken to prepare for the lecture?
- Were the notes helpful?
- Were the visual aids clear and easy to read?
- What steps could be taken to improve preparation and presentation?
- Did the questions stimulate discussion?
- Were the purposes of the presentation achieved?
- How did the students react?

The distribution of questionnaires to the class is a more formal way of evaluating a lecture. Many such forms have been designed and can usually be obtained from the teaching unit within your institution. An example of such a form designed by one of us is included at the end of the chapter. The questions asked have been derived from research on effective teaching. However, like all such forms its main limitation is that it cannot present answers to all the questions **you** may think are relevant. Accordingly, you should consider adding to or adapting such forms to your own special needs.

The best way of obtaining an independent evaluation is to seek the services of a teaching unit. They will sit in on your lecture and prepare a detailed analysis. They might also suggest that they record the presentation on video or audiotape and go back over it with you later.

A CONCLUDING THOUGHT

It may be objected that the crowded curriculum does not allow time for the techniques described in this chapter. This objection rests on the argument that material has to be 'covered'. However, it assumes that students will learn that material. This is unfortunately not the case as we have already shown that levels of attention to a traditional expository lecture decline, and it is known that other indicators of performance – such as recall and even pulse rates – fall fairly rapidly around 20 minutes after the lecture begins. Worse, what little is learned in the remainder of the lecture time interferes with understanding earlier material. So perhaps the question you should be asking yourself is 'Should I be wasting time speaking for 50 minutes?'

The problem of enhancing student learning is unfortunately much more complex than this (see also Chapter 8). In some courses it is the case that few students regard lectures as an important learning activity. Further, lecturers are perceived as being a means to pace study, as a way of keeping in touch with the coursework, and as supplementary to other more important learning activities such as practical classes, tutorials and assignments. At worst, lectures are seen as a boring waste of time relieved only by the skill and daring of the paper plane throwers and other attention seekers.

The challenge is to work out a clear and educationally defensible rationale for lecturing. Another challenge is to lecture effectively and efficiently. Lecturing can be a useful learning method for students where the techniques of teaching large groups are appropriately employed. Also, it can be a personally rewarding and interesting task for academic staff. We hope that this chapter has contributed to dealing with these challenges.

GUIDED READING

Almost all books which are concerned with the practicalities of teaching in education will devote some space to the lecture and you will undoubtedly find many of these helpful.

Perhaps the most popular book on lecturing is Donald Bligh's

What's the Use of Lectures?, Penguin, Harmondsworth, Middlesex, UK, 1972. Most libraries will have this publication which is, unfortunately, out of print. (A later edition is available from the author at Briar House, Clyst Honiton, Exeter EX5 2LZ, Devon, UK.) Bligh's book gives an overview of the research, useful information on preparing and delivering lectures, and an interesting section on alternatives to the lecture.

A very practical book that can be recommended is George Brown's *Lecturing and Explaining*, Methuen, London, UK, 1978. This book is full of exercises and suggested activities that you can carry out for yourself or with a colleague. Some chapter headings will suggest the flavour of the book: 'Learning to lecture', 'Preparing and designing explanations' and 'Helping students learn from lectures'.

Lecturing (HERDSA Green Guide No 7) by Robert Cannon also provides clear practical advice, in more detail than provided in this chapter, on preparation, presentation, evaluation and active learning methods. (It is available from the Higher Education Research and Development Society of Australasia, C/- Tertiary Education Research Centre, University of New South Wales, Kensington, NSW 2033, Australia.)

A very useful book to review for ideas on improving learning from lectures is *53 Interesting Things to Do in Your Lecture* by G Gibbs, S Habeshaw and T Habeshaw, Technical and Educational Services, 37 Ravenswood Road, Redlands, Bristol BS6 6BW, UK, 1985.

Books and journals referred to in this chapter:

Use Your Head by T Buzan, BBC Publications, London, 1974.

'Evaluating the effectiveness of lectures' by B Cooper and J M Foy, *Universities Quarterly*, **21**, 1967.

Teaching Tips: A Guidebook for the Beginning College Teacher (7th Ed) by WJ McKeachie, Heath, Lexington, Massachusetts, USA, 1978.

The University of Adelaide
Advisory Centre for University Education

STUDENT EVALUATION OF TEACHING

This questionnaire seeks information about your experience of this teacher and this course.

Please answer each question accurately. If you feel you cannot answer a particular question leave it out and go to the next question. Your responses are anonymous.

Circle the number which most closely corresponds to your view about each statement.

Thank you for your assistance with this evaluation.

COURSE.. LECTURER..

PART A

1 How do you feel about the content of this course?

Very Positive	Positive	Neutral	Negative	Very Negative
1	2	3	4	5

2 All things considered, how would you rate this staff member's effectiveness as a university teacher?

Very Poor	Poor	Satisfactory	Good	Very Good
1	2	3	4	5

3 How would you describe the workload in this course?

Very Light	Light	Reasonable	Heavy	Very Heavy
1	2	3	4	5

4 The pace at which this course is being presented is...

Too Fast	Fast	About Right	Slow	Too Slow
1	2	3	4	5

5 How would you describe the degree of difficulty of this course?

Very Easy	Easy	Reasonable	Difficult	Very Difficult
1	2	3	4	5

PART B

Please indicate the extent to which you agree or disagree with the following statements by circling the appropriate number.

	Strongly Agree	Agree	Uncertain	Disagree	Strongly Disagree
Course Characteristics					
6 I understand the subject matter	1	2	3	4	5
7 This course is being poorly co-ordinated	1	2	3	4	5
8 The course is challenging	1	2	3	4	5
9 Assessment methods are fair	1	2	3	4	5
10 Course materials are well prepared	1	2	3	4	5
11 Proposed aims of course are being implemented	1	2	3	4	5
12 I am learning something valuable	1	2	3	4	5
13 Recommended readings contribute to understanding in the course	1	2	3	4	5
Teacher Characteristics					
14 Communicates effectively	1	2	3	4	5
15 Teaching style makes note-taking difficult	1	2	3	4	5
16 Enthusiastic about teaching this course	1	2	3	4	5
17 Stimulates my interest in this subject	1	2	3	4	5
18 Interested in students	1	2	3	4	5
19 Accessible to students outside classes	1	2	3	4	5
20 Encourages students to express ideas	1	2	3	4	5
21 Well organised	1	2	3	4	5
22 Confident	1	2	3	4	5
23 Clear explanations given	1	2	3	4	5

PART C

24 What improvements to the course, or to the teaching, could you suggest?
Please PRINT your comments, to preserve anonymity, on the back of this sheet.

Thank you for answering this questionnaire. Please return it as directed.

Chapter 2 Making a Presentation at a Conference

INTRODUCTION

This chapter may appear to be out of place in a book about education and teaching. However, most teachers, at some time, will wish to make a presentation at a conference or professional meeting, and there are many obvious similarities between large group teaching and presenting a paper. There are also significant differences which may not be quite so obvious which made us feel that this chapter might be appreciated.

Poster sessions are growing in popularity at many national and international meetings as an alternative to the formal presentation of papers. We have, therefore, included a short section on the preparation of a conference poster.

In due course, you will be asked to take on the responsibility of chairing a conference session. This also has its pitfalls so a section on this topic concludes the chapter.

PRESENTING A PAPER

Though much of the advice given in the chapter on large group teaching is just as relevant in this section, the aims of a meeting or conference are different enough to warrant separate consideration. Much of this difference relates to the restriction on time. It is likely that a strict time limit will be imposed. If you are in the position to give a paper it is certain that you will have a lot to say, far more in fact than can possibly be delivered in the time allocated. You will also be caught in the difficult situation of many of the audience being unfamiliar with the details of your area of interest, some of the audience knowing considerably more than you do about the area, and all of the audience likely to be critical of the content and the presentation. These and other factors make the giving of a paper a pressure situation, particularly for the young and inexperienced hoping to make a good impression on peers and superiors. However, it is also a situation that is amenable to resolution by careful planning and attention to technique.

PREPARING THE PAPER

There are three stages that you must go through during the preparation of a conference paper. These stages are:

- the collection and selection of information and data;
- the arrangement (getting the structure right and deciding on the most suitable presentation);
- polishing, writing it out and rehearsal.

The collection and selection of the data

There is a great tendency for speakers to cram more than is possible into their papers with the inevitable consequence of either speaking too fast or going over time. The audience is primarily interested in hearing a short, cohesive account of your ideas or research. To achieve this you are not going to be able to present all your hard-won data. You are going to have to be very selective and in most instances you will have to restrict yourself to only one aspect of your work. Your first step should be to write down in one sentence the main purpose of your paper. In other words, what is the main message you wish to get across? Having done this you should identify the three or four pieces of evidence you will use to give support to your views. You should keep in mind that you will only have two or three minutes to describe each piece of work so that when you are assembling your data you must be aware of the need to simplify the results into a more easily digested form (eg complex tables reconstructed into histograms).

The arrangement

The first task is to get the basic plan worked out. The presentation will fall into several components. For a research paper, a basic plan might look like this:

- Introduction
- Statement of the purpose of your research

- Description of methods and results
- Conclusions

The introduction: This is a vital component. It must set the context of your work for the audience, many of whom may not be experts in your field. They may also be suffering the after-effects of the previous paper or of a dash from another concurrent session venue. You have no more than two minutes to excite the interest of the audience before they relapse into the mental torpor so prevalent at conferences. You must therefore give a considerable amount of thought to the introduction. It must be simple, precise and free from jargon. It must start from a broad base so that the audience can identify the point at which your research fits into the discipline and make them appreciate the vital importance of your own contribution.

The statement of purpose: This should take no more than a minute but it is also a vital component of the talk. In these few sentences you will need to convince the audience that what you set out to do was worthwhile. It should flow from the introduction so that it sounds like a logical outcome of previous research.

The description of methods and results: The description of methods will usually have to be abbreviated or even reduced to a mention ('The so-and-so technique was used to ...'). If the development of a new method is an important part of your work then it must obviously be described in more detail but you must decide whether the main message is to relate to the method or the results subsequently obtained.

The results are usually the most important part of the paper. You will inevitably have spent a lot of time getting them together. It is possible that you have already prepared a variety of tables, graphs and charts for the purpose of publication. Do not fall into the trap of thinking that these are suitable for presentation to a live audience. How often have you, for example, sat in a meeting where someone has projected slides of an incomprehensible and illegible table or a wall of prose taken straight from a journal?

The conclusions: These must flow naturally from the results of your work. You will be aiming to make one or two clear statements which you are able to conclude from your work. It is advisable to be reasonably modest in your claims.

The presentation aids: The second task is to prepare the visual aids, and possibly handouts, to support your paper. In most instances these will be slides or overhead transparencies. Considerable thought must be given to these as their impact and quality may make or break the presentation. They must complement your oral presentation, not duplicate it. The technical aspects of the preparation of slides and overhead transparencies are covered in greater detail in Chapter 7, which deals with teaching aids, but a few specific points are worth mentioning at this time.

Having roughed out the plan of the talk it should be reasonably obvious where a slide (or transparency) is required. You may need one or two during the introduction to stimulate interest.

The slides or overheads of the results provide you with the greatest challenge. It is during this part of your paper that the visual material will often be of more importance than the verbal ('A picture says a thousand words'). Avoid complex tables and where possible convert tables to charts or simple graphs. Rarely is it appropriate to show masses of data; just show the mean or rounded-off figures. If you feel you really must refer to complex data it is better to have this prepared in printed form and available to the audience as a handout.

Having prepared the visual aids, check that they are accurate and legible. (As a rule, a slide where the information can be read with the naked eye will be satisfactory when projected. Lettering on an overhead transparency must be no less than 5 mm high.) Then take them to a large lecture theatre and project them. Check that they are indeed legible from the furthermost corners of the theatre. It is also helpful to take a colleague with you to check that the message is clear and that there are no spelling mistakes.

Polishing, writing it out and rehearsal

At this stage you should have a good idea of what you intend to

say and of the aids that you require. It is now advisable to write the text of the talk in full. Do not write in the style you use for journal publications. Pretend you are talking to an individual and write in a conversational mode, avoiding jargon wherever possible.

As you go along, identify the correct position for the aids. As you do this you may find places where you have not prepared an appropriate slide or overhead. Remember, during the talk the visual aids and handouts must complement your talk and not distract from it. There must always be an accurate match between the content of your aids and what you are saying. When using slides, if you do not have one which illustrates what you are saying, insert a blank slide. This will also avoid the distracting practice of saying 'slide-off' and 'slide-on'. If you intend to use the same slide more than once get multiple copies made to avoid the confusion that will ensue if you ask the projectionist to go back to a previous slide.

Once you have the rough draft, edit it. Then read it aloud at about the pace you think you will go during the presentation. Further editing and alterations will be required, as almost certainly you will have gone over time. Some find it a useful ploy at this stage to record the talk on a tape-recorder and listen to the result very critically.

The next stage is to present the paper to an honest and critical colleague. The feedback is often extremely valuable.

You must now decide whether you will read the paper or not. Most authorities consider that you should be well enough rehearsed to speak only with the aid of cue cards or the cues provided by your visual aids. If you have a highly visual presentation most of the audience will be looking at the screen so the fact that you are reading is less critical. Providing the text is written in a conversational style, and you are able to look up from your text at frequent intervals, then reading is not a major sin. The chief risk of speaking without a text in a very short presentation is going over time which, at best, will irritate the chairman and the audience, and, at worst, will result in your being cut-off in mid-sentence.

Whatever you decide, rehearsal is essential and a dress rehearsal in front of an audience (eg your department) a week or two before the event is invaluable. Not only will you receive comments on the presentation but you will also be subject to questions, the answering of which, in a precise manner, is just as important as the talk itself. Remember that the quality of your material and its presentation is a public reflection of the quality of your department and institution. So a proper dress rehearsal is very desirable.

PREPARING THE ABSTRACT AND YOUR CONTRIBUTION TO THE PROCEEDINGS OF THE CONFERENCE

The abstract

Most conferences will require you to prepare an abstract, sometimes several months before the meeting. Initially, it may be used to help select contributions and, ultimately, will be made available to participants. Contributors are often tardy in preparing their abstracts which is discourteous to the conference organizers and makes their task more difficult.

The abstract should be an advertisement for your paper. It should outline the background to the study and summarize the supporting data and the main conclusions. Quite frequently, abstracts promise what they do not deliver so avoid being guilty of false advertising.

The proceedings

Many national and most major international conferences will publish proceedings. Should you be presenting a paper at such a conference you will be required to provide your contribution to these proceedings during the conference or shortly afterwards. It is not appropriate to present the organizers with the script and slides that you have just used in your presentation. The contribution to the proceedings should be written in a style consistent with that used in a journal article. The content should be the same as in the presented paper but not necessarily identical. It is perfectly permissible to expand some areas, particularly with regard to the methods and results sections, where more detail could be included. This should all be done within the guidelines for format and length specified by the organizers.

WHAT YOU SHOULD DO ON THE DAY

'There's many a slip 'twixt cup and lip.' This saying provides a reminder that, however good your preparation for the presentation of the paper has been, there is still plenty that can happen to ruin your carefully laid plans. Fortunately, many such problems can be prevented or anticipated. You should find it helpful to work your way through the checklist shown in Figure 2.1.

FIGURE 2·1 CHECKLIST TO USE ON THE DAY OF THE PRESENTATION

Before the presentation

★ Check your slides and overheads to see that they are in the correct order, labelled in this order and slides spotted in the correct place (see Figure 7.5).

★ If possible, load your slides into an empty magazine of the type to be used during your presentation. Project them somewhere to check that they are indeed in the correct order and the right way around. Then seal the magazine and label it with your name.

★ Seek out the projectionist and explain your plan for the slides and the arrangements for lighting.

★ Check your prompt cards or text.

★ Check the venue and the operation of slide and overhead projectors. You may be expected to operate the lights, a slide changer and a light pointer. Have a practice during a break in the programme.

★ If you are expected to use a microphone check how it is attached or adjusted.

★ Try and sit in on a talk in the same venue early in the day to get a feel for the acoustics and how you should use the audiovisual facilities.

During the presentation

- Walk confidently to the podium and arrange your cards or text. Adjust the microphone and set out the position of pointers, overhead transparencies, slide changers and so on to your satisfaction.
- Commence your talk with an appropriate opening (eg 'Mr Chairman, ladies and gentlemen').
- Present the opening few sentences without reference to any notes, looking around the audience without fixing your eye on any particular individual, however friendly or prestigious that person may be.
- Call for the lights to be dimmed (or do it yourself) when your first slide is to appear. Never turn off the lights completely unless it is absolutely essential and in any case only for a minimum of time. On the other hand do not continually call for 'lights on' or 'lights off'. Your slides should have been designed to be clearly visible in subdued light.
- Speak at a rate which sounds slow to you – it will not be too slow for the audience. Try and use more emphasis than seems natural to your own ear – again, it will not sound too theatrical to the audience. Let your enthusiasm show through by using suitable hand and facial gestures.
- If you turn to the screen to point something out make sure you do not move away from the microphone. This is a particular problem with a fixed microphone, in which case move behind it so that you continue to speak across it.
- When you come to the conclusion, say so ('In conclusion I have shown …' or 'Finally, …').

Handling questions

Most conferences have a fixed period of time for questions. In some ways this is the most critical part of the presentation. Some people in the audience are going to test you out with penetrating questions and how you handle them will enhance or detract from the impact of your performance. This is one of the reasons why we suggested a full dress rehearsal in front of your department in order to practise your answering of difficult questions and to avoid leaving weaknesses in your arguments for which some participants may be searching. Figure 2.2 lists some points to remember.

FIGURE 2.2
POINTS TO REMEMBER WHEN HANDLING QUESTIONS

- Listen to the question very carefully.
- If the question is complex or if you have any concern that not all the audience heard it, restate it clearly and succinctly.
- Answer the question politely and precisely. Sometimes a simple 'yes' or 'no' will be sufficient. Avoid the danger of using the question to give what amounts to a second paper.
- Be alert to the questioners who are deliberately trying to trick you or to use the occasion to display their own knowledge of the subject.
- If the question is particularly awkward or aggressive try to deflect it as best you can. Strategies include agreeing with as much of what was said as possible, acknowledging legitimate differences of opinion or interpretation, or suggesting you meet the questioner afterwards to clarify your position. At all costs avoid a heated head-on clash in front of your audience. However, do not be afraid to politely disagree with any questioners, however eminent, when you are sure of your ground. Remember, they may only be testing you out!

PREPARING A CONFERENCE POSTER

The conference poster is a popular alternative to presenting papers at conferences. You will find that the poster has several advantages over the traditional paper such as:

- allowing readers to consider material at their own rate;
- being available for viewing over an extended period of time;
- enabling participants to engage in more detailed discussion with the presenter than is the case with the usually rushed paper discussion session.

If the conference organizers have arranged a poster session we suggest that you consider taking advantage of it. It may provide you with an opportunity to present additional material to the conference that would otherwise be difficult because of limitations on the number of speakers.

What is a conference poster?

A conference poster is a means of presenting information on a static display. A poster should include at least the following parts:

- A title
- An abstract
- Text and diagrams
- Name of author(s), their address(es) and where they may be contacted during the conference

Additional materials that you might consider for the poster, or in support of the poster, include:

- Illustrations
- Exhibits and objects
- Audiovisual displays, such as a synchronized tape–slide presentation or videotape
- A take-away handout, which might be a printed reduction of your poster
- A blank pad, so that when you are not in attendance interested readers can leave comments or contact addresses for you to follow-up

Preparing the poster

If you decide that a poster is an appropriate way of presenting your information, there are a number of things you must take into consideration during its preparation.

Firstly, ascertain from the conference organizers the facilities that will be available. Then proceed to plan the poster. The poster should communicate your message as simply as possible, so do not allow it to become clogged with too much detail. Layout ideas can be gleaned by looking through newspapers and magazines or, better still, from graphic design books and journals. If possible, discuss these ideas with a graphic artist. The layout should be clear, logical and suitable for the material being presented. Try a number of different rough layouts first and seek the opinion of a colleague to determine the best. A possible layout is shown in Figure 2.3.

FIGURE 2.3
POSSIBLE LAYOUT FOR A CONFERENCE POSTER

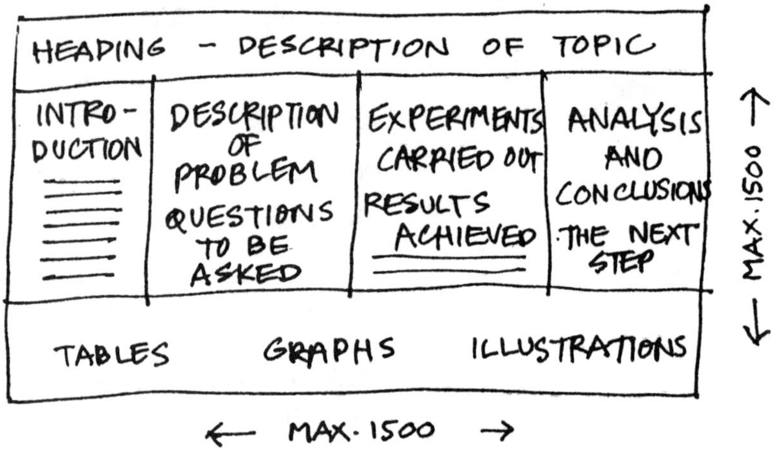

5MM LETTERS

Text lettering should be large enough to be read at the viewing distance, which is likely to be about one metre. In this case, we suggest that the smallest letters be at least 5 mm high and preferably larger. Titles and text can be prepared by using a suitable software package on a microcomputer, or by using Letraset or a lettering machine that produces large and bold characters. For detailed text, a clear typed or printed sheet can be photographically enlarged. Make sure that diagrams are bold enough to be seen easily and consider using colour to highlight significant points.

Break up the density of text into several discrete parts. For example, consider dividing the text into an abstract, an introduction, a statement of method, results and conclusion – each with its own clear heading. A short list of references or of publications arising out of your work might also be appropriate. Remember that in preparing your poster you are really trying to achieve many of the same things you would wish to achieve with a talk or lecture: to attract attention, maintain interest and to generally communicate effectively.

CHAIRING A CONFERENCE SESSION

Much of the success of a conference will depend on the quality of the chairing of individual sessions. Should this task fall to you, there are many responsibilities to fulfil. There are three categories of task – responsibilities to the organizers, to the speaker and to the audience.

Responsibilities to the organizers

The organizers of the conference will have approached you several months before the event. If you are lucky, they will also have given you detailed guidelines to follow but, if not, you must, at a minimum, find out:

- the time and length of the session;
- the number, names and addresses of the speakers;
- a copy of the instructions given to speakers, with particular reference to the time allocated for the presentation and the time allocated for discussion;
- whether there are concurrent sessions.

Ideally, you will contact the speakers in advance of the conference to ensure they have indeed received instructions and understand the implications, particularly with regard to time. You may find that some are inexperienced and nervous about the prospect of their presentation and your advice will be appreciated. Referring the speaker to the earlier parts of this chapter might be valuable.

If early contact has not been made, it is essential to meet with speakers before the session. You must clarify the format of the session and reinforce your intention to stick rigidly to the allocated time. You should explain the method to be used to indicate when there is one minute to go, when time is up and what steps you will take should the speaker continue for longer than 10–15 seconds over time. This may sound draconian but, believe us, it is vital. A timing device on the lectern is an invaluable aid to compliance.

Before the session, you must also familiarize yourself with the layout of the venue, the audiovisual facilities and the lighting. In the absence of a technician, you may be called on to operate the equipment and lighting or to instruct the speakers in their use.

At the start of the session, announce that you intend to keep to time – and do so.

Finally, you must be certain that the session and individual presentations commence and finish at the programmed time. This is particularly important when there are concurrent sessions.

Responsibilities to the speakers

Speakers invariably fall into one of three categories:

The well-organized speakers: These will tell **you** exactly what they are going to do and what they require. If you ask them how long they are going to speak, they will tell you in minutes and seconds! You will need to have little concern for these speakers, but they will expect you to be as well-prepared and organized as themselves.

The apprehensive speakers: These will generally be younger and less experienced. They will often have a well-prepared paper to present but are in danger of not doing themselves justice. You can assist such speakers greatly by familiarizing them with the facilities before the session and encouraging them to practise operating the audiovisual equipment. If this seems beyond them, you may be able to take on the task yourself. Calm reassurance that all will be well is the message to convey.

The confident under-prepared speaker: These are remarkably prevalent and the most dangerous for the chairperson. They will not seek advice and will deny having received detailed instructions about their presentation. When you ask them how long they expect to speak, you will receive an off-hand response. This will tell you that they have not rehearsed their presentation and will almost certainly go over time. There is little you can do to help such people because they are certain that they have everything under control. However, they can be your downfall unless you prepare to intervene. Before the session you must convince them that you are serious about cutting them off if they speak over time. Unfortunately, this strategy will often fail and you must be prepared to act immediately the first time a speaker goes over the allotted time. After a maximum of 15 seconds grace, rise from your chair. If the hint is not immediately taken, you have no option but to politely but firmly stop the speaker. Examples can be cited of such speakers being physically led off the stage still talking, but such extremes should not arise! Fortunately, you will only have to intervene in such a way once in a session and, should it happen, your future as an invited chairperson is assured.

In the discussion period you must see fair play. Ensure that questions are relevant and brief. Do not allow questioners to make long statements or commence a minipresentation of their own work. Suggest that any significant differences of opinion be explored informally at the subsequent coffee-break.

Responsibilities to the audience

The audience has a right to expect several things from the chairperson. They must be able to hear the speaker and see the slides. They must be reassured that you will keep the speakers to time to protect their opportunity to ask questions and to allow them to move to concurrent sessions. Speakers going over time is the commonest complaint of participants and the chairperson is usually held to blame. During the question period you should ensure that the time is not monopolized by the intellectual heavies in the front rows. On the other hand you must also be well prepared to ask the first question if none is immediately forthcoming from the audience.

Finishing off

At the close of the session, thank the speakers and the audience. Also remind them of the starting time of the next session. You may also have been asked to transmit information from the organizers. Particularly important would be to obtain completed evaluation forms for the session if these were provided.

GUIDED READING

The book we recommend for further reading on scientific presentations is Calnan and Barabas' *Speaking at Medical Meetings*, Heinemann, London, 1972. This pocket-sized do-it-yourself guide is not only valuable but entertaining. It also contains many useful illustrations and good advice about the preparation of visual aids.

With regard to the preparation of posters, a helpful reference is *Static Displays – Posters, Wallcharts, Exhibits in Medical Education*, Council for Educational Technology, London, 1973.

An excellent general text on public speaking is C Turk's *Effective Speaking*, Spon, London, 1985. This is a comprehensive reference work that has been written by a university lecturer. You should consider obtaining a copy for your personal library.

Chapter 3 Teaching in Small Groups

INTRODUCTION

This chapter assumes you have been asked to teach a small group. It also assumes that the group you are to take will meet on more than one occasion and therefore will present you with the opportunity to establish and develop a productive group atmosphere. Small group teaching can be a most rewarding experience. However, to achieve success you will need to plan carefully and to develop skills in group management. You should not fall into the common error of believing that discussion in groups will just happen. Even if it does, it is often directionless, unproductive, unsatisfying and perhaps threatening. To avoid these problems you will need some understanding of how groups work and how to apply a range of small group techniques to achieve your goals.

THE IMPORTANCE OF SMALL GROUP TEACHING

Teaching in small groups enjoys an important place among the teaching methods commonly found in education for two rather different reasons. The first of these can be described as **social** and the other as **educational**. For many students in higher education, and especially those in the early years of their studies, the small group or tutorial provides an important social contact with peers and teachers. The value of this contact should not be underestimated as a means for students to meet and deal with people and to resolve a range of matters indirectly associated with your teaching, such as difficulties with studying, course attendance and so on. Such matters will, of course, assist with the attainment of the more strictly educational objectives of your course.

Among the educational objectives that you can best achieve through the use of small group teaching methods are the development of higher-level intellectual skills such as reasoning and problem-solving, the development of attitudes, and the acquisition of interpersonal skills such as listening, speaking, arguing and group leadership. These skills are important to all students who will eventually become involved with other professionals, the community, learned societies and the like. The distinction between social and educational aspects of small group teaching is rather an arbitrary one but it is important to bear it in mind when you plan for small group teaching.

WHAT IS SMALL GROUP TEACHING?

Most of what passes for small group teaching turns out to be little more than a lecture to a small number of students. Nor is size, within limits, a critical feature for effective small group teaching. We believe that small group teaching must have at least the following three characteristics:

- Active participation
- Face-to-face contact
- Purposeful activity

Active participation

The first, and perhaps the most important, characteristic of small group teaching is that teaching and learning are brought about through discussion among **all** present. This generally implies a group size that is sufficiently small to enable each group member to contribute. Research and practical experience have established that between five and eight students is ideal for most small group teaching. You will know that many so-called small groups or tutorial groups are very much larger than this ideal. Although a group of over 20 students hardly qualifies as a small group, it is worth remembering that, with a little ingenuity, you can use many of the small group teaching procedures described in this chapter with considerable success with larger numbers of students. Generally speaking, though, in such a situation you will be looking for a technique which allows you to break the number down into subgroups for at least some of the time.

Face-to-face contact

The second characteristic of small group teaching is that it involves face-to-face contact among all those present. You will find it difficult to conduct satisfactory small group teaching in a lecture theatre or tutorial room with students sitting in rows. Similarly, long boardroom-type tables are quite unsuitable because those present cannot see all other group members, especially those seated alongside. Effective discussion requires communication which is not only verbal but also non-verbal, involving, for example, gestures, facial expressions, eye contact and posture. This will only be achieved by sitting the group in a circle.

Purposeful activity

The third characteristic of small group teaching is that the session must have a purpose and must develop in an orderly way. It is certainly not an occasion for idle chit-chat although, regrettably, some teaching in groups appears to be little more than this. The purposes you set for your small group can be quite wide. They include discussing a topic or a problem, and developing skills such as a criticizing, analysing, problem-solving and decision-making. It is highly likely that you will wish the small group session to achieve more than one purpose. In universities and colleges, most groups are expected to deal with a substantial amount of content. However, you will also wish to use the small group approach to develop the higher intellectual skills of your students and even to influence their attitidues. To achieve these various purposes you will need considerable skills in managing the group and a clear plan so that the discussion will proceed in an orderly fashion towards its conclusion.

MANAGING A SMALL GROUP

Small group teaching is considerably more difficult to manage than a lecture because you must take a closer account of the students' behaviour, personalities and difficulties. To achieve success with a small group you must also have a clear understanding of how a group operates and how it develops. You have particular responsibilities as the initial leader of the group but your role will vary considerably, both within a session and from session to session. For instance, if you adopt an autocratic or authoritarian style of leadership (not an uncommon one) you may well have a lot of purposeful activity but there will be a limited amount of spontaneous participation. You should preferably adopt a more co-operative role where you demonstrate an expectation that the students will take responsibility for initiating discussion, providing information, asking questions, challenging statements, asking for clarification and so on. A successful group is one that can proceed purposefully without the need for constant intervention by the teacher. This is hard for most teachers to accept but is very rewarding if one recognizes that this independence is one of the key goals of small group teaching and is more important than satisfying one's own need to be deferred to as teacher and content expert.

In managing a group there are two main factors that have to be considered. These are those relating to the **task** of the group and those relating to the **maintenance** of the group. In addition there must be a concern for the needs of each student within the group.

The tasks of the group: Tasks must be clearly defined. This is something that must be high on the agenda of the first meeting. The reason for the small group sessions and their purpose in the course must be explained. In addition, you must initiate a discussion about how you wish the group to operate, what degree of preparation you expect between group meetings, what role you intend to adopt, what roles you expect the students to assume and so on. Because such details may be quickly forgotten it is desirable to provide the student with a handout. Figure 3.1 lists some headings which may be helpful.

FIGURE 3.1
SUGGESTED HEADINGS FOR A SMALL GROUP HANDOUT

- Course title, description and aims.
- Teacher's name and availability.
- List of students' names.
- How the group is to run (eg teacher's role, students' roles, method to be used).
- Work requirements (eg assignments, case presentations).
- Assessment arrangements.
- Reading matter.

Maintenance of the group: This refers to the achievement of a good 'climate' for discussion. It must be one that is open, trusting and supportive rather than closed, suspicious, defensive and competitive. It is important to establish that the responsibility for this factor rests with the students as well as with the teacher. The firm but pleasant handling of the loquacious or dominating students early in the session or the encouragement of the quiet student to contribute are examples of what must be achieved to produce the required environment for effective group discussion.

The successfully managed group will meet the criteria shown in Figure 3.2.

FIGURE 3·2
CRITERIA FOR A GOOD GROUP
(AFTER HILL, 1982)

- Prevalence of a warm, accepting, non-threatening group climate.
- Learning approached as a co-operative rather than a competitive enterprise.
- Learning accepted as the major reason for the existence of the group.
- Active participation by all.
- Equal distribution of leadership functions.
- Group sessions and learning tasks are enjoyable.
- Content adequately and efficiently covered.
- Evaluation accepted as an integral part of the group's activities.
- Students attend regularly.
- Students come prepared.

STRUCTURE IN SMALL GROUP TEACHING

We mentioned earlier the need to have a clear plan so that the group discussion will proceed with purpose and in an orderly fashion. A structured approach to the task and the allocation of the time available is a useful tool for you to consider. A simple example of such a structured discussion session is illustrated in

Figure 3.3. This approach will be particularly helpful when students new to your course may not know how to interpret your simple direction to 'discuss'. The approach is suggested for any course where a reading task has been set.

FIGURE 3-3
STRUCTURED CASE DISCUSSION SESSION

1	PRELIMINARIES / HOUSEKEEPING MATTERS	5 MINS
2	A STUDENT PRESENTS THE INITIAL HISTORY AND EXAMINATION FINDING OF ONE OF HIS WARD PATIENTS	5 MINS
3	GROUP ASKED TO GENERATE HYPOTHESES AND DIAGNOSES, DISCUSS IMMEDIATE MANAGEMENT AND INITIAL INVESTIGATIONS	15 MINS
4	INFORMATION PROVIDED ON WHAT THE STUDENT (AND CONSULTANT) THOUGHT WAS THE DIAGNOSIS, WHAT WAS DONE, AND WHICH INVESTIGATIONS WERE ORDERED. GROUP DISCUSSES ANY DISPARITIES	10 MINS
5	STUDENT PRESENTS FURTHER DATA ON INVESTIGATIONS AND PROGRESS. GROUP DISCUSSES ANY DISPARITIES	10 MINS
6	GROUP LEADER OFFERS CONCLUDING REMARKS AND OPPORTUNITY FOR CLARIFICATION OF UNRESOLVED ISSUES	5 MINS
	TOTAL	50 MINS

Note that the structure lays out **what** is to be discussed and how much **time** is budgeted. Such a scheme is not intended to encourage undue rigidity or inflexibility, but to clarify purposes and tasks. This may seem to be a trivial matter, but it is one which creates considerable uncertainty for students. Keeping to a time budget is very difficult. You need to be alert to how time is being spent and whether time from one part of the plan can be transferred to an unexpected and important issue that arises during discussion.

Another structure is illustrated in Figure 3.4. This structure includes the principle of 'snowballing' groups. From an individual task, the student progresses through a series of small groups of steadily increasing size. There are special advantages in using this structure which are worth noting: it does not depend on prior student preparation for success; the initial

FIGURE 3.4
A SNOWBALLING GROUP DISCUSSION (AFTER NORTHEDGE)

INDIVIDUAL WORK	STUDENTS READ BRIEF BACKGROUND DOCUMENT ON TOPIC, READ CASE HISTORY AND EXAMINE LABORATORY RESULTS.	10 MINS
WORK IN PAIRS	STUDENTS COMPARE UNDERSTANDINGS, CLEAR UP DIFFICULTIES, MAKE PRELIMINARY DIAGNOSIS AN DECIDE ON FURTHER TESTS	10 MINS
WORK IN SMALL GROUP	PAIRS REPORT TO THE SMALL GROUP. GROUP DISCUSSES DIAGNOSES AND FURTHER TESTS, SEEKING AGREEMENT OR CLARIFYING DIS-AGREEMENTS. GROUP PREPARES REPORT FOR WHOLE GROUP	15 MINS
REPORTING BACK TO WHOLE GROUP	EACH SMALL GROUP PRESENTS REPORT, TEACHER NOTES MAIN POINTS ON BOARD, BUTCHERS PAPER OR OVERHEAD TRANSPARENCY. AS GROUPS CON-TRIBUTE, TEACHER AND STUDENTS OFFER COM-MENTS. TEACHER OR STUDENTS ATTEMPT SUM-MARY OF POINTS RAISED AND SOME FORM OF CONCLUSION.	20 MINS

individual work brings all students to approximately the same level before discussion begins; and it ensures that everyone participates, at least in the preliminary stages.

For teachers of science students there is a wealth of stimulating examples of small group teaching methods in the book *Small Group Teaching in Undergraduate Science* by Black. In one section of this book, which discusses the teaching of intellectual skills, a broad structure is recommended, as shown in Figure 3.5.

FIGURE 3.5
STRUCTURED SESSION FOR TEACHING INTELLECTUAL SKILLS (AFTER BLACK)

- ★ A set of prepared problems.
- ★ A group large enough to be divided for part of the time into four subgroups of about four students each.
- ★ Subgroups working for about half the time on the problems.
- ★ A brief report on the work of each group.
- ★ Class discussion based on the group's reports.

WHEN THINGS GO WRONG

You will undoubtedly have a variety of difficulties to deal with in your group sessions. For example, you might decide to ignore the behaviour of a sleeping student or an amorous couple in the back row of a lecture class, providing it was not disruptive, but it would be impossible to do so in a small group. How you resolve problems with the working of the group is critical. An authoritarian approach would almost certainly destroy any chance of establishing the co-operative climate we believe to be essential. It is generally more appropriate to raise the problem with the group and ask them for their help with a solution.

One of your main roles as a group leader is to be sensitive to the group and the individuals within it. Research has identified a number of difficulties that students commonly experience. These are connected with:

- making a contribution to the discussion;
- understanding the conventions of group work and acceptable modes of behaviour;
- knowing enough to contribute to the discussion;
- being assessed.

These difficulties frequently get in the way of productive discussion. They tend to be due to genuine confusion on the part of students, combined with a fear of exposing their ignorance in front of the teacher and their peers. It is therefore essential for you to clarify the purpose of the group and the way in which students are to enter into the discussion. Their previous experience of small group sessions might lead them to see the occasion as only a threatening question-and-answer session. They must learn that ignorance is a relative term and that their degree of ignorance must be recognized and explored before effective learning can begin. A willingness by the teacher to admit ignorance and demonstrate an appropriate way of dealing with it will be very reassuring to many students.

Confusion in the student's minds about how they are being

assessed can also cause difficulties. Generally speaking, assessing contributions to discussion is inhibiting and should be avoided. If you do not have discretion in this matter then at least make it quite clear what criteria you are looking for in your assessment. Should you be able to determine your own assessment policy then the following criteria are worth considering:

- require attendance at all (or a specified proportion of) group meetings as a prerequisite;
- set formal written work, eg a major essay, a series of short papers, a case analysis;
- set a group-based task, eg keeping an account of the work done by the group.

The teacher's perceptions of group difficulties may not necessarily match those of the students. A discussion with the group about how they think things are going or the administration of a short questionnaire are ways of seeking feedback.

Once the group is operating it is important to be continually on the look out for trouble. You must be sensitive to the emotional responses of the group and to the behaviour of individual students. Bion has categorized group responses into fight, flight, pairing and dependency. These categories serve to highlight some of the common features in groups which hinder their successful operation.

Fight: This appears in several forms. It may be easily recognized as overt hostility and aggression but equally damaging can be misplaced humour, quibbling over semantics, point-scoring and attempting to establish intellectual superiority. Teachers are as frequently guilty of such activities as their students.

Flight: Students become very adept at avoiding difficult situations. In our experience this is one of the biggest problems in small groups. It may take the form of withdrawal from active participation, by distracting behaviour, or by attempting to change the direction of the discussion without the resolution of a sticky problem.

Pairing: A pair within the group may carry on a more or less personal conversation for considerable periods of time. All too often the teacher is one of them. A good group will not allow this but in many groups the majority of the discussion may be carried on by only a small minority of students.

Dependency: This is also a common problem and is one which may be present in a whole group. The group avoids tackling problems by getting someone to do it for them. This may be the brightest student or most frequently the teacher who may even be flattered into it. Some students seem to be particularly adept at this and their teachers particularly susceptible.

INTRODUCING STIMULUS MATERIALS

A very useful means of getting discussion going in groups is to use what is generally known as 'stimulus material'. We have seen how this was done in the snowballing group structure described previously. The range of stimulus material is really very large indeed. It is limited only by your imagination and the objectives of your course. Here are a few examples:

- A short multiple-choice test (ambiguous items work well in small groups).
- A case study.
- A trigger film or video (eg short open-ended situation, such as a person-to-person encounter).
- A patient in a medical or dental course.
- Observation of a role-play.
- Visual materials (eg photographs, slides, specimens, real objects, charts, diagrams, statistical data).
- An audio-recording (eg an interview, sounds, a segment of a radio broadcast).
- A student's written report on a project, field-work or laboratory-work.

- A journal article or other written material, such as an abstract. (The paper by Moore gives an interesting example of this approach using extracts from literary works to help students understand the broader cultural, philosophical, ethical and personal issues of the subject under study. The added benefit, of course, is a broadening of the educational experience of students.)

ALTERNATIVE SMALL GROUP DISCUSSION TECHNIQUES

As with any other aspects of teaching it is helpful to have a variety of techniques at one's fingertips in order to introduce variety or to suit a particular situation. Such techniques include:

- One-to-one discussion
- Buzz groups
- Brainstorming
- Role-playing
- Evaluation discussion

One-to-one discussion

This is a very effective technique which can be used with a group of almost any size. It is particularly useful as an 'ice-breaker' when the group first meets, and is valuable for enhancing listening skills. It can also be used to discuss controversial or ethical issues so that forceful individuals with strong opinions will be prevented from dominating the discussion: they will also be required to listen to other opinions and express them to the whole group. (See Figure 3.6.)

FIGURE 3.6
CONDUCTING A ONE-TO-ONE DISCUSSION

A **Procedure**

- Group members (preferably including the teacher) divide into pairs and each person is designated 'A' or 'B'.
- Person A talks to person B for an **uninterrupted** period of 3–5 minutes on the topic for discussion.
- Person B listens and avoids prompting or questioning.
- Roles are reversed with B talking to A.
- At the conclusion the group reassembles.
- Each person, in turn, introduces themselves before introducing the person to whom they were speaking. They then briefly paraphrase what was said by that person.

B **Use as ice-breaker**

- Group members are asked to respond to a question such as 'Tell me something about yourself' or 'What do you expect to learn from this course?'

C **General use**

- Group members respond to appropriate questioning, eg 'What is your opinion about . . .?'

It is useful to insist on the no interruption rule (though not so much when used as an ice-breaker). Prolonged periods of silence may ensue but person A will be using this time for uninterrupted thinking, a luxury not available in most situations. Often the first superficial response to a question will be changed after deeper consideration.

Buzz groups

These are particularly helpful to encourage maximum participation at one time. It is therefore especially useful when groups are large, or if too many people are trying to contribute at once or, alternatively, if shyness is inhibiting several students. (See Figure 3.7.)

FIGURE 3.7
CONDUCTING A BUZZ GROUP

Procedure

- The group is divided into subgroups of 3–4 students.
- Discussion occurs for a few minutes (the term 'buzz' comes from the hive of verbal activity!).
- A clear task must be set.
- Each group reports back to the whole group.

Brainstorming
This is a technique that you should consider when you wish to encourage wide and creative thinking about a problem. It is also valuable when highly critical group members (including perhaps yourself?) appear to be inhibiting discussion. If used frequently, it trains students to think up ideas before they are dismissed or criticized. The key to successful brainstorming is to separate the generation of ideas, or possible solutions to a problem, from the evaluation of these ideas or solutions. (See Figure 3.8.) Before using brainstorming, we suggest you have a look at Stein's book on creativity.

FIGURE 3.8
CONDUCTING A BRAIN-STORMING SESSION

Procedure

- Explain these rules of brainstorming to the group:
  - criticism is ruled out during the idea generation stage;
  - all ideas are welcome;
  - quantity of ideas is the aim (so as to improve the chances of good ideas coming up);
  - combination and improvement of ideas will be sought once all new ideas are obtained.
- State the problem to the group.
- A period of silent thought is allowed during which students write down their ideas.
- Ideas are then recorded (in a round-robin format) on a blackboard, overhead transparency or butcher's paper for all to see.
- When **all** ideas are listed, and combination and improvement of ideas are complete, discussion and evaluation commences.

Role-playing

This is a powerful and underused technique. It is very valuable in teaching interpersonal communication skills, particularly in areas with a high emotional content. It has been found to be helpful in changing perceptions and in developing empathy. It is not a technique to use without some experience so you should arrange to sit in on a role-play session before using it in your own course. In this regard, colleagues teaching psychology, education, psychiatry or counselling should be able to help you. (See Figure 3.9.)

FIGURE 3.9
CONDUCTING A ROLE PLAY

Procedure

- Explain the nature and purpose of the exercise.
- Define the setting and situation.
- Select students to act out roles.
- Provide players with a realistic description of the role or even a script. Allow time for them to prepare and, if necessary, practise.
- Specify observational tasks for non-players.
- Allow sufficient time for the role-play.
- Discuss and explore the experience with players and observers.

Plenary session

In many group teaching situations, and indeed at conferences and workshops, subgroups must report back to the larger group. This reporting back can be tedious and often involves only the subgroup leaders who may present a very distorted view of what transpired. The plenary session method may help you get round these problems. (See Figure 3.10.)

FIGURE 3.10
CONDUCTING A PLENARY SESSION

Procedure

- Subgroups sit together facing other subgroups.
- The chair of subgroup A briefly reports the substance of the discussion in subgroup A.

- The chair of subgroup B then invites members of subgroups B, C, D etc to ask questions of any member of group A.
- After 10 minutes chair B reports on the discussion in subgroup B and the process is repeated for each subgroup.
- The 10 minute (or other) time limit must be adhered to strictly.

Evaluation discussion

From time to time during a course it is desirable to review the progress of your small group, including the teaching methods and the material you are covering. There are a number of ways you could collect information about these matters, one of which is the technique called the evaluation discussion. (See Figure 3.11.)

FIGURE 3.11
CONDUCTING AN EVALUATION DISCUSSION

Procedure

- Before the group meeting students are asked to write a 1–2 page evaluation of the group's work focusing equally on their reactions to the **processes** of teaching and **what** they are learning.
- Each student reads this evaluation to the group.
- Each member of the group is then free to ask questions, agree or disagree, or to comment.

For success you must be sure to create an atmosphere of acceptance where negative as well as positive information can be freely given. Listen rather than react!

EVALUATING SMALL GROUP TEACHING

Evaluation implies collecting information about your teaching and then making judgements based on that information. Making judgements based on what one student says, or on rumour or intuition, is simply not good enough. You must collect information in a way that is likely to lead to valid judgements. However, constant evaluation of small group activities is not recommended as it may inhibit the

FIGURE 3·12
EXAMPLE OF TUTORIAL QUESTIONNAIRE
(ADVISORY CENTRE FOR UNIVERSITY EDUCATION, UNIVERSITY OF ADELAIDE)

Name .... **Course**..

Please indicate your thoughts about the tutorial given by this particular tutor. Your responses are anonymous.

Indicate your present thoughts by means of a tick on the four-point scale.

(A) **The tutor**

good group leader	----	poor group leader
fits into the group	----	too forceful
likes opinions questioned	----	discourages the questioning of opinions
patient	----	impatient
never sarcastic	----	sarcastic
lively	----	monotonous
pleasant manner	----	unpleasant manner
interested in students	----	not interested in students
interested in my ideas	----	not interested in my ideas
interested in me as an individual	----	does not know me
encourages me to discuss problems	----	unable to discuss problems
treats me as an equal	----	treats me as a subordinate
clearly audible	----	mumbles
stresses important material	----	all material seems the same
makes good use of examples and illustrations	----	never gives examples
explanations clear and understandable	----	quite incomprehensible
appears confident	----	not confident

(B) **The tutorials**

well organized	----	muddled
good progression	----	poor progression
well prepared	----	not well prepared
time well spent	----	a waste of time
new material covered	----	merely repeat lecture material
have thrown new light on lecture course	----	irrelevant to understanding of lecture course
overcome difficulties encountered in lectures	----	difficulties not dealt with

(C) **The student's response**

I am fully aware of my progress	----	I seems to be 'working in the dark'
I enjoy contributing	----	I try to say nothing
I look forward to the tutorials	----	I would prefer not to attend
I have learnt a lot	----	I have learnt nothing
I am more inclined to continue with the subject	----	I have developed an aversion to the subject

Advice or suggestions for the future should be written on the back.

development and working of the group. Evaluation may be of two types: informal or formal.

Informal evaluation: This can proceed from your careful reflection of what happened during your time with the group. You may do this by considering a number of criteria which you feel are important. For example, you may be interested in the distribution of discussion among group members, the quality of contribution, the amount of your own talk, whether the purpose of the session was achieved and so on. Of course, your reflections will be biased and it is wise to seek confirmation by questioning students from time to time. However, the importance of informal evaluations lies in your commitment to turn these reflections into improvements. If you are concerned with your own performance, the assistance of a trusted and experienced colleague sitting in on the group, or even just a discussion of your own feelings about the group, may be very helpful.

Formal evaluation: One formal approach to evaluation has already been described, the evaluation discussion. Other approaches include the use of questionnaires and the analysis of video-recordings of the group at work. Standard questionnaires are available which seek student responses to a set number of questions. An example is shown in Figure 3.12.

Although such standard questionnaire can be useful, you may find it more beneficial to design one that contributes more directly to answering questions which relate to your own course and concerns. As questionnaire design is a tricky business, it is recommended that you seek the assistance of a teaching unit. The analysis of videotapes of your group at work is also a task which would require the expertise of someone from a teaching unit or a relevant teaching department such as psychology.

GUIDED READING

For a wide-ranging discussion of the purposes and techniques of small group teaching we suggest you turn to the collection of papers edited by D Bligh: *Teach Thinking by Discussion*, SRHE/NFER-Nelson, Guildford, UK, 1986. This monograph also provides a good introduction to the research literature on small groups.

If you are looking for brief, practical guides to the use of discussion in small groups, you might find it helpful to obtain a copy of W F Hill's *Learning Thru Discussion*, Sage, Beverley Hills, California, USA, 1982 and J Lublin's *Conducting Tutorials* (Green Guide No 3), Higher Education Research and Development Society of Australasia, C/- Tertiary Education Research Centre, University of New South Wales, Kensington, NSW 2033, Australia, 1987. The outlines in these books will help you get started if you are new to small group teaching. You will, of course, need to adapt some of the strategies to the circumstances of your own teaching.

Another excellent guide, to both the theory and the practice of group work, is D Jacques, *Learning in Groups*, Croom Helm, London. 1984.

Books and journals referred to in this chapter:

Experiences in Groups by W R Bion, Tavistock, London, 1968.

'Medical humanities – a new medical adventure' by A R Moore, *New England Journal of Medicine*, **295**: 1479–80, 1976.

'Learning through discussion at the Open University' by A Northedge, *Teaching at a Distance*, **2**: 10–17, 1975.

Small Group Teaching in Undergraduate Science by P J Black *et al*, Nuffield Foundation/Heinemann, UK, 1977.

Chapter 4 Teaching Practical and Laboratory Classes

INTRODUCTION

Practical and laboratory classes are usually regarded as an essential component of science-based courses. They are also found in some arts-related disciplines (eg geography, languages, psychology). In this chapter, we will try to identify those objectives which are best achieved in practical classes and discuss the ways in which you can assist your students to achieve them. This is important as studies have shown that student reactions to practical work are variable. There are several possible reasons for this. One important reason may be that the running of practical classes is often left to junior staff who do not have the experience or authority to recognize and rectify deficiencies. This is often not their fault as staff training in laboratory class supervision is rarely provided. Designing, implementing and running a practical course is perhaps the most complex, and certainly the most expensive, component of the curriculum and needs the skill and support of senior staff.

To make the best use of the resources available for practical work we strongly suggest you obtain a copy of *Teaching in Laboratories* by Boud, Dunn and Hegarty-Hazel upon which we have drawn liberally for the material in this chapter.

THE ATTRIBUTES OF AN EFFECTIVE PRACTICAL CLASS TEACHER

These have been identified on the basis of the opinions of experts, the perceptions of students, and from the observation of actual teaching. As the role of the teacher seems to be particularly critical in the laboratory setting if the aims of such courses are to be achieved, you may find it salutary to check yourself against these attributes.

- Do you encourage active participation by students and avoid having them stand around in an observational capacity?
- Do you have and demonstrate a positive attitude to your teaching?
- Is the emphasis of your teaching on critical thinking, problem-solving, aspects of scientific enquiry and other intellectual activities which require the students to think?
- Do you encourage students to focus on the integration of the practical exercises with the learning of material taught in other components of the course?
- Do you supervise students closely enough to recognize those having difficulties with the concepts on which the exercises are based?
- Do you provide adequate opportunities for your students to practise their skills?
- Do you provide a good role model?
- Does your teaching provide stimulation and challenge?
- Are you friendly, helpful and available to your students?

Should your honest answer to some of these questions be 'no' then you are probably a typical teacher, as research has shown that these desirable attributes are rarely all present. Just being aware of these attributes should encourage you to be more critical of your approach.

The remainder of this chapter will deal with some of the ways which could enhance your effectiveness when teaching in the laboratory.

THE PURPOSES OF PRACTICAL AND LABORATORY TEACHING

The purpose of practical and laboratory classes will vary somewhat depending on whether the course is primarily for students of the discipline (eg chemistry for chemistry students) or is a service course for another department or faculty (eg

chemistry for engineering students). If you are teaching your own students, the emphasis will be on the fundamentals of the discipline. Not surprisingly, perhaps, most teachers will find it easier to relate to this situation than to adapt to service course teaching where the expectation is to teach only those aspects of the discipline which are relevant to the client department or faculty. Teachers may feel less well motivated to this task, with potential serious consequences for the students. If you find yourself in such a situation you must liaise with your colleagues from the client area and attempt to get an understanding of their specific needs. If you take the trouble to do so you may find it is a more interesting and challenging experience than you had anticipated.

While there may be many and varied objectives for practical teaching, or more specifically laboratory-related teaching, the only two that can be said to be best achieved in this setting are:

- Learning practical skills and techniques relevant to the discipline
- Understanding the process of scientific enquiry

Learning practical skills and techniques

The laboratory is the place where organized opportunities can be provided for students to appreciate and practise a range of skills and techniques which someone graduating from the course would be expected to acquire. These basic skills and techniques should be defined so that students have a clear idea of what is expected. Such skills are best stated in terms of what the student should have achieved at the end of the course (known as behavioural objectives). An example might be: 'At the end of the class the student will be expected to set up and operate a ... (particular piece of equipment)'.

Understanding the process of scientific enquiry

This is obviously something fundamental to the teaching of science and clearly the practical class is potentially one of the most valuable opportunities for the students to acquire such an understanding. Yet research has consistently shown that many courses which would espouse this purpose fail dismally in its achievement. The reasons for this are many but include a lack of planning and inappropriate teaching strategies. It is important to clarify what the process of scientific enquiry means in your discipline and what activities the students can perform which will enable them to develop the necessary insights and skills. The general headings are likely to include the following:

- Critical analysis of the literature
- Identifying and grappling with set or novel problems
- Analysis and interpretation of experimental data
- Written and verbal communication

COURSE PLAN AND TEACHING METHODS

It is to be hoped that the practical classes are well integrated into an overall course plan and that this is readily available to you and to the students. Unfortunately this is not always the situation. If a plan is not available, you should try to generate one using the procedures suggested in Chapter 5 on curriculum planning. It is helpful to have a plan which identifies the aims of the course and from which you can identify those aims which are to be achieved in the practical classes as opposed to lectures and tutorials. You may then find that the current classes are not meeting the expected objectives either in breadth or in depth. This is because many practical courses have evolved over time in an *ad-hoc* way rather than being planned or constantly upgraded on the basis of course evaluation.

The assessment of **breadth** will come from having a defined series of topics and skills which the students are expected to cover and acquire. The assessment of **depth** is more difficult and requires an honest and critical appraisal of the content of the laboratory exercises. This may reveal that the intellectual effort required by the student is about the same as following a recipe in a cookbook when you were hoping that they were attaining skills in the process of scientific enquiry. In their book, Boud, Dunn and Hegarty-Hazel classify laboratory activities into three types depending on the purpose:

- Controlled exercises
- Experimental investigations
- Research projects

Controlled exercises

These are exercises wholly devised by staff. The main purpose is to help students develop fundamental skills and techniques which have to be mastered. These exercises can usually be completed in one session and the procedures are detailed in a laboratory manual. Such exercises are most appropriate early in a course when new skills must be acquired before more advanced work can be undertaken. (See Figure 4.1.)

FIGURE 4.1 PROCEDURE FOR CONDUCTING A CONTROLLED EXERCISE

Procedure

- Define the objectives of the exercise ('At the end of the class you will be able to ...').
- Identify reading material to be given to students before the class.
- Provide a detailed account of the procedure to be followed by students.
- Identify and provide all laboratory materials and equipment.
- Specify the observations that have to be made.
- Describe the nature of the report required for assessment purposes.

Figure 4.2 gives an example of such a controlled exercise.

Experimental investigations

The principal characteristic of this type of exercise is the provision of an opportunity for students to display some initiative and exert an element of choice in the design and conduct of the experimental work. The idea is to simulate, albeit still in a controlled and limited way, the process of scientific enquiry. The problems selected should be a natural extension of the students' previous understanding and experience. Such an activity could extend over several classes. It

FIGURE 4.2
EXAMPLE OF A CONTROLLED LABORATORY EXERCISE (ADAPTED FROM HEGARTY-HAZEL, 1988)

OBJECTIVE	REFERENCE MATERIAL	LABORATORY ACTIVITIES
AT THE END OF THIS CLASS THE STUDENT WILL BE ABLE TO COLLECT AND APPROPRIATELY EXAMINE A MID-STREAM SPECIMEN OF URINE (MSU)	LECTURE NOTES AND HANDOUTS; TEXT REFERENCES. DETAILS OF PROCEDURES FOR COLLECTION AND ANALYSIS IN LABORATORY MANUAL	1. THE PATIENT IS YOU. COLLECT AN MSU 2. CHECK pH, PROTEIN AND OTHER BIOCHEMICAL TESTS USING THE DIP STICKS. 3. EXAMINE SPECIMEN MICROSCOPICALLY 4. PLATE SPECIMEN AND INCUBATE FOR 24 HOURS 5. HAVE YOUR TUTOR CHECK YOUR PROCEDURES 6. RECORD RESULTS

might aim to relate only to one aspect of the process of scientific enquiry. For example, the students might be provided with a novel problem and asked to generate a series of possible hypotheses and experiments without any expectations that the experiments would ever be performed. On the other hand students could be provided with experimental data and asked to analyse and interpret these even though they had not themselves performed the experiments. (See Figure 4.3.)

FIGURE 4.3
PROCEDURE FOR CONDUCTING A CONTROLLED LABORATORY EXERCISE

Procedure

★ Define the objectives of the exercise.

★ Identify a series of problems which incorporate the subject area of interest.

★ Devise a series of research questions of a limited nature (eg 'What is the effect of changing pH and temperature on the growth characteristics of the bacteria provided?').

★ Provide or suggest background resource materials.

- Provide the range of equipment and materials necessary to solve the set problem tasks.
- Describe the nature of the report required for assessment purposes.

An example of an experimental investigation is shown in Figure 4.4.

FIGURE 4.4
EXAMPLE OF AN EXPERIMENTAL INVESTIGATION (ADAPTED FROM HEGARTY-HAZEL, 1988)

OBJECTIVE	CASE STUDY	LABORATORY
AT THE END OF THIS CLASS THE STUDENT WILL BE ABLE TO DIAGNOSE THE CLINICAL PROBLEM USING APPROPRIATE EXAMPLE OF A LABORATORY INVESTIGATION AND TO PROVIDE A REPORT.	A 26 YEARS OLD WOMAN GAVE A HISTORY OF LOWER ABDOMINAL PAIN ASSOCIATED WITH FREQUENCY AND BURNING SENSATION ON MICTURITION. NO PREVIOUS TREATMENT HAD BEEN GIVEN. TEMPERATURE WAS NORMAL. MICROSCOPIC EXAMINATION OF THE URINE REVEALED 160x 10^6 WHITE BLOOD CELLS/LITRE AND NO CASTS. BIOCHEMICAL TESTING SHOWED NO PROTEIN AND NO GLUCOSE.	1. EXAMINE THE URINE PROVIDED AND MAKE A DIAGNOSIS. 2. WRITE OUT THE LABORATORY FORM THAT SHOULD BE SENT TO THE TREATING DOCTOR. 3. WHAT OTHER MICROBIOLOGICAL INVESTIGATIONS SHOULD BE CONDUCTED BEFORE THE LABORATORY REPORT CAN BE COMPLETED?

Devising such exercises requires considerable skill. It is important to monitor what students are actually doing in order to be certain that the aims are being met. If done well, such activities will have a strong motivational effect.

Research projects

Research projects have always held an important place in science-based courses, particularly at the honours or doctorate level. There is now a growing appreciation of the value of research projects, often of a more limited and less technically demanding nature, at an earlier phase of tertiary education. Projects provide the student with a real-life experience of research which is quite different to the more controlled exercises described previously. They are highly motivational to most students because of the high level of active participation, the close contact with supervisors and research staff, the lower emphasis on assessment and the greater degree of personal responsibility.

Research projects can be undertaken individually, by groups, and by attachment to a research team with the student accepting responsibility for certain aspects of an established project. Whatever the approach, the role of the supervisor is critical. Should this be your role the points outlined in Figure 4.5 should be remembered.

FIGURE 4·5
TASKS FOR THE SUPERVISOR OF A RESEARCH PROJECT

Procedure

- Meet with the student and agree on the objectives of the exercise and the problem to be researched.
- Work out a schedule of work covering the period during which the project is to be conducted, with provisional deadlines for completion of each stage (eg literature review; hypothesis generation and experimental design; experimental work; data analysis; report).
- Arrange a regular meeting time with student to check progress (remember the task is to guide not direct).
- Assist the student to prepare the final report or to give the seminar presentation by means of critical discussion and practice. (Students could be referred to the appropriate sections in this book!)

Research has shown that supervisors vary markedly in their commitment and skill. It is recommended that departments using research projects should provide guidelines and training for supervisors. Several valuable publications are available which could be used or modified for this purpose (see under Guided Reading at the end of the chapter).

Alternative methods

A combination of modern technology and interest in new teaching techniques has provided alternatives to the conventional approaches to practical work already discussed. Two of the most well-established have been called the personalized system of instruction (PSI) or Keller plan and the audio-tutorial. These approaches should be particularly considered when large classes are a problem. Microcomputers are now being increasingly used as a laboratory tool, providing both opportunities for the analysis of data and for simulation.

The personalized system of instruction (PSI): This is one of the approaches to teaching which has been well studied and shown to be equal, or superior, in appropriate circumstances to conventional methods. In essence, it consists of a series of well-designed modules which usually replace part or all of a lecture or laboratory course. Each module has clearly stated behavioural objectives and a variety of prescribed learning activities with clear assessment goals which have to be achieved before moving on to the next module. The originator of this approach, Keller, identified the key features as self-pacing and mastery learning.

This approach has been used in many science-based courses, including physics, chemistry and various biological sciences. It is usually to be seen in the early phases of a course where basic skills and knowledge need to be mastered. Expertise is required to implement this method and you will require the full support of your department if you are to succeed. Initially you should seek help from someone with experience or from the teaching advisory service in your institution.

The audio-tutorial method: This is another useful and flexible method which may also be a valuable adjunct to practical classes. Activities are usually carried out in a carrel equipped with a tape-recorder and other audiovisual devices such as a slide projector. There may, in addition, be other materials and equipment which the student will have to use and this would be particularly so in a practical teaching situation. Such material need not necessarily be located in the carrel. The essence is again one of student self-pacing with support sessions being held individually or in small groups with a tutor, perhaps once or twice a week.

As with PSI, some expertise is required in clarifying objectives and designing and preparing the tutorial and material. However, the approach is not a difficult one to master. The chapter on preparing teaching materials and aids provides additional advice which should be helpful, particularly the section on tape–slide presentations (Chapter 7, pages 142-4). This gives an example from one of our own audio-tutorials on electrocardiography which incorporates basic knowledge, interpretation and the practical undertaking of a recording which students have to present to a tutor with their report. An example from a biochemistry laboratory course, as developed by one of our colleagues, is referred to in the guided reading. If you are planning to embark on a programme of audio-tutorial development we strongly recommend that you look at the book by Brewer.

Computer-aided instruction (CAI): The ubiquitous microcomputer is bringing into the range of all teachers the possibility of introducing CAI into their courses. This is particularly relevant in practical teaching, as a wide range of computer simulations are available which can provide opportunities for students to undertake activities which otherwise might be too complex (eg analysis of experimental data, management games), too expensive (eg design and testing of architectural structures) or too dangerous (eg dealing with emergency situations in medicine; observing the effects of experimental changes of physiological variables). The possibilities are only limited by the imagination of the designers. Unfortunately, unless you are a computer expert, the task of developing such simulations will be beyond your capabilities. The best approach is to find out whether such simulations are already available in your discipline and, if so, where they are being used. If possible, arrange a visit to try out the material and see if it is suitable for use in your particular course. Only then should you purchase the package.

Computers can also be used as another variation of the PSI with the computer managing the activities of students, perhaps even including the assessment. However, more expertise is required to establish such a system than with the written or tape-based approaches. An example from our own institution in biochemistry is cited in the references (Parslow, 1984).

ASSESSMENT

The principles for assessing practical work are the same as for any other component of the course and are discussed in detail in Chapter 6. Here we only wish to draw your attention to some specific issues in assessing practical work. First, it is important to ensure that the method of assessment matches the objectives. If for instance, the objective is to learn to use a piece of equipment or develop a new skill then these must be observed and evaluated against some criteria of achievement that have previously been agreed. On the other hand, if the objective is to have the student develop some aspect of scientific thinking, then the method must require the student to demonstrate this approach. This may sound self-evident but there is plenty of research to show that laboratory and project reports often fail to measure those aspects of higher-level thinking which practical work is uniquely placed to assess.

Feedback is another area of assessment that is frequently under-used. Student learning will be greatly facilitated by feedback on their performance and every opportunity should be taken to provide this in written form (eg constructive comments on laboratory reports), by group and individual contacts with staff, or by structured reports of the kind illustrated in Chapter 6 on assessment.

PUTTING IT TOGETHER

A checklist for the development of a laboratory course which you may find helpful is given in Figure 4.6 on p 68.

FIGURE 4.6 CHECKLIST FOR DEVELOPING A LABORATORY COURSE

- What are the overall goals?
- What are the specific aims for the course/class?
- What are the behavioural objectives for the session and are they written down?
- What tasks must students perform?
- What teaching strategies are to be used?
- How is the course to be sequenced?
- What pre-laboratory requirements are there and how are students to achieve them?
- What post-laboratory work is to be required?
- What form of assessment is to be used and what weight will it receive in relation to other components of the course/curriculum?
- How will the course be monitored?

GUIDED READING

The most useful book we have found on practical teaching is the one we have referred to frequently in this chapter; it is both a scholarly review of research on practical teaching and a source of valuable detailed advice: *Teaching in Laboratories* by D Boud, J Dunn and E Hegarty-Hazel, SRHE/NFER-Nelson/Open University, Milton Keynes, UK, 1986.

A recent and detailed account of individualized work in laboratories that we can recommend is *Learning More and Teaching Less: A Decade of Innovation in Self-Instruction and Small Group Learning* by Ilma Brewer, SRHE/NFER-Nelson, Guildford, UK, 1985. This is a very thorough account of the use of the audio-tutorial and groups in courses in the natural sciences.

Another interesting source of detailed advice and ideas is *Practical Work in Undergraduate Science* edited by Jon Ogborn and published for the Nuffield Foundation by Heinemann, London, 1977. This book is part of a series that was developed in the Higher Education Learning Project (Physics). Another useful title in the same series, which takes up the ideas of PSI and the audio-tutorial, is *Individual Study in Undergraduate Science* edited by W Bridge and L Elton, 1977.

For guidance in supervising research work, we suggest you consult *Supervising Postgraduates* (Green Guide No. 3) by Ingrid Moses, Higher Education Research and Development Society of Australasia, C/- Tertiary Education Research Centre, University of New South Wales, Kensington, NSW 2033, Australia, 1985; and also the references cited in it. Though mainly directed at the postgraduate, ideas presented can be adapted for undergraduate research projects.

Articles referred to in this chapter:

'Microcomputers and other educational hardware: a department's experience' by G Parslow, *Biochemical Education*, **12**: 157–61, 1984.

'Prior learning, challenges and critical thinking in the medical student laboratory' by E Hegarty-Hazel. In *The Medical Teacher*, K R Cox and C E Ewan (Eds), Churchill-Livingstone, Edinburgh, 1988.

Chapter 5 Curriculum Planning

INTRODUCTION

This chapter aims to assist you when you become involved in some way in curriculum planning and wish to do so in a systematic manner. Unfortunately, there is no straightforward formula to guide you in this activity. The reasons for this are as follows. First, curriculum planning is a complex business involving more than purely educational considerations. For example, you will find that full account must be taken of the political and economic context in which you teach. Lucky is the planner who can rely on the full co-operation of the teaching staff, has an adequate budget and does not have to take account of departmental or faculty politics. Second, relatively few courses are started from scratch. Much curriculum development must inevitably be a matter of revising and adapting existing courses or materials. And third, there are important differences between individuals - especially between individuals working in different disciplines - in the ways in which they view a variety of educational issues. You may, for instance, see your main function as transmitting appropriate knowledge, skills and attitudes. On the other hand you may perceive your role as being primarily concerned with the personal and social development of your students as well as with their intellectual development. In a book of this kind it is not possible to provide a theoretical discussion which can fully take into account these various orientations. However, we believe that you should be aware of these differences and we would encourage you to read further on the matter to help develop your own particular orientation and your own approach to curriculum development. Our reference to Miller and Seller at the end of this chapter is a useful starting point for your reading.

In our view, the key to curriculum planning is to forge educationally sound and logical links between planned intentions, course content, teaching and learning methods, and the assessment of student learning while taking full account of student characteristics. Too many courses start with vague intentions, consist of teaching which has a tenuous relationship to these intentions and employ methods of assessment which bear little or no relationship to either. Such courses then place students in the unfortunate situation of playing a guessing game, with their academic future as the stake! This pattern can be improved by adopting an approach which links the intentions with course content, teaching, and the assessment. These elements of curriculum planning, together with a consideration of students, are the focus of this chapter.

Curriculum development should be an ongoing process. In practice, curriculum development can and does start with any of the linked elements named above and we have no desire to alter that practice. Indeed, our major concern is to ensure that each element – intentions, teaching, assessment, content – **is** considered and that the links between the elements are thoughtfully made.

WHO SHOULD BE RESPONSIBLE FOR CURRICULUM PLANNING?

Although we assume you have some responsibility for curriculum planning it is unlikely that this will be a solo affair. You will have additional resources on which to draw which may include staff in your own and related departments, staff of a university teaching unit, members of your discipline outside your immediate environment, and students. These people may form a planning committee or a panel of advisers. Whatever your situation, experience suggests that some form of consultation with others is very desirable.

COURSE CONTENT

Content is a broad concept meant to include all aspects of knowledge, skills and attitudes relevant to the course **and** to the intellectual experiences of students and their teachers in a course.

While not always easy to achieve, we feel that course content should be made explicit and that this will then put you in a better position to make informed and coherent decisions in your curriculum planning. There are several different criteria for selecting content that may be more or less relevant to your work. These criteria are presented below for your consideration.

Philosophical criteria

These criteria focus attention on theoretical, methodological and value positions. For example:

- Content should be a means of enhancing the intellectual development of students, not an end in itself.
- Content that is solely concerned with technical matters has no place in a university education; content must also involve moral and ethical considerations.
- Content should contribute to a deep rather than to a surface view of knowledge.

Professional criteria

These criteria recognize that courses in the professions may reflect explicit legal and professional requirements before practice is permitted:

- Content must provide the kinds of theoretical and practical experiences required for registration.
- Content should include attention to professional ethics.

Psychological criteria

These criteria relate to the application of psychological principles – especially of learning theory – to teaching:

- Content should be carefully integrated to avoid fragmentation and consequential loss of opportunities for students to develop 'deep' approaches to learning (see Chapter 8).
- Content selection must provide opportunities to emphasize and to develop higher-level intellectual skills such as reasoning, problem-solving, critical thinking and creativity.
- Content should relate to 'process' activities and to the development of attitudes and values.

Practical criteria

These criteria concern the feasibility of teaching something and may relate to resource considerations:

- Content may be derived from one or two major texts because of a lack of suitable alternative materials.
- Content could be influenced by the availability of a 'key' teaching resource: library materials, computer equipment, people, patients, physical environment, etc.

Student criteria

These criteria relate to the characteristics of the students you teach. We consider these criteria to be so important in curriculum planning that a full section is devoted to them. Student criteria may affect the choice of content in a variety of ways:

- Content may be selected to reflect the needs and interests of the group.
- Content should be matched to the intellectual and maturity level of students.

  Content might take account of the diverse life experiences of students.

How you actually go about selecting content will largely be determined by the kind of person you are (especially by your views about the relative importance of your role as a teacher, the role of students and course content) and by the norms and practices in the discipline you teach. Keep in mind, of course, that much of this selection process is often applied unconsciously.

STUDENTS

Taking account of student characteristics, needs, and interests is the most difficult part of curriculum planning. The reason for this is that teachers now face increasingly heterogeneous groups of students and, at the same time, must take account of legislative requirements to address specific issues such as equal opportunity. It is no longer enough to state that curriculum planners need to 'take account of students' and then to proceed as if they did not exist. This process may be quite formal and even negotiated between a staff member and students. For instance, in most graduate programmes, and in some humanities and social science undergraduate courses, topics and assessment arrangements are decided in a consultative fashion. On the other hand, student influence may be less explicit but nevertheless very powerful, especially, for example, in professional courses where students may convey their impatience with basic science or theoretical coursework that are perceived as irrelevant yet are a prerequisite for subsequent study.

'Taking account' of students is partly your responsibility and partly your institution's responsibility. Institutional responsibilities – which we would encourage you to influence positively – might include:

- the provision of special physical facilities to assist handicapped students in courses;
- tutorial assistance in the English language, especially for non-native speakers;
- bridging courses (for knowledge and skill deficiencies) and foundation courses (to assist in the process of adjustment to higher education).

Your responsibilities are no less onorous. In addition to accommodating the wide range of personalities, learning styles, social backgrounds, expectations and academic achievement of normal or direct-entry students from school you must also be prepared to teach students from other backgrounds and with 'different' characteristics than your own. Four examples of current concern which we will briefly discuss are: women, mature-age students, first-year students and overseas students.

Women students

The role of women and women students in higher education has received a lot of attention. In curriculum planning you should consider:

- The selection of suitable course content that at least acknowledges that women comprise half the human race: thus, the selection of women writers in English courses, feminist perspectives in history, and the work of women in science and technology are matters for attention.

- The elimination of sexist language in course materials and in teaching.

You will be aware that many governments now view these issues as so important that there are legal sanctions for transgressions. As your institution is likely to have formal policies relating to women, you should seek out this information and relate it to your curriculum planning.

Adult (maturè-age) students
This group brings a rich diversity of experiences, problems and possibilities. Older students usually approach higher education with a greater intensity of purpose than their younger peers because so much more, in terms of sacrifices and ambitions, rests on their study and achievements. They also expect staff to be more flexible and adaptive in their teaching and assessment methods. These students often experience anxiety over assessment arrangements. Vagueness on your part, or in the course plan, can only contribute to this concern.

First-year students
The teaching of this group is of particular concern because of their need to adjust to the learning environment of higher education. Some students will belong to a group with specific needs (eg mature-age or overseas students). The sensitive use of small group work (see Chapter 3) can be a means of dealing with some matters, but not all. The selection of content – taking care to induct students into the language and peculiarities of your subject and to the assessment methods – and above all, the clarity of your expectations can all contribute to a smooth and successful transition.

Overseas students
Overseas students, especially those in their first year of studies, require special consideration. These considerations relate most closely to matters of your personal preparation for teaching. Two important aspects of preparation are your own level of cultural awareness and the way in which you teach. Cultural awareness can be developed through training programmes, but

a more realistic approach for the busy teacher is to develop out-of-class contact with relevant overseas student groups and through reading. The usual principles of good teaching apply as much for this group as for others but particular care should be given to your use of language - especially your speed, pronunciation and use of unnecessarily complex sentence constructions.

As you review these considerations for each group of students you will probably realize that almost all are worthwhile principles for planning and teaching **all** students and should therefore be taken into account in routine curriculum planning. The issue of 'taking account' of students is underscored by the jibe one often gets in discussions on this subject: 'What do you do for female, mature-age, first-year students from overseas?' There is, of course, no simple answer to this question and little research which bears directly on the problem of teaching mixed groups in higher education. If pressed, we would offer the following general suggestion: Be aware of your own attitudes and behaviour, be available and helpful to **all** students and, particularly, be willing to learn, to adapt and to adjust. A tall-order, we know. But elsewhere in this book you will find suggestions on ways of developing these qualities. Of particular relevance is Chapter 8 on student learning. To assist you further, we have recommended rather more reading in this chapter to highlight our belief that you should take particular note of your students when planning a course of study for them.

As we remarked in our introduction, there is no straightforward formula to guide you in curriculum planning. Nowhere is this more evident than in the process of linking the many content and student considerations we have been discussing to the particulars of preparing a course plan. We suggest that you prepare a simple checklist of content and student matters to be taken into account during the next step of curriculum planning - writing course objectives.

AIMS AND OBJECTIVES

The intentions of the course are usually expressed in the form of aims and objectives. Aims will reflect the teacher's orientation to education, and be general statements of intent. Objectives are rather more specific statements of what students should be able to do as a result of a course of study. We are convinced that clear objectives are a fundamental tool in curriculum development because they make the rational choice of content, and teaching and learning activities, possible and are important in planning a valid assessment. Objectives provide a guide to teachers and to students, but should not be so restrictive as to prevent the spontaneity that is so essential to the higher education of students. The relationship between objectives, teaching and learning activities, and assessment is best set out in a course planning chart such as that seen in Figure 5.1.

FIGURE 5·1
EXAMPLE OF A COURSE PLANNING CHART

OBJECTIVES	TEACHING AND LEARNING ACTIVITIES	ASSESSMENTS
AT THE COMPLETION OF THE COURSE THE STUDENT WILL BE ABLE TO:		
1 TAKE A COMPREHENSIVE HISTORY	1 PRECEPTOR SESSIONS WITH REVIEW OF VIDEO RECORDINGS OF PATIENT INTERVIEWS	1 PRECEPTOR'S JUDGEMENT BASED ON VIDEO RECORDING OF A HISTORY AT THE END OF COURSE
2	2	2
3	3	3

Each defined objective is matched with appropriate teaching and learning activities and with a valid form of assessment. For instance, in the example, you would not expect the students to learn to be able to 'take a comprehensive history at the completion of the course' on the basis of lectures, nor would you expect that this could be validly assessed by a paper-and-pencil test. The course designer has provided a relevant teaching and learning activity and a suitable form of assessment.

WRITING OBJECTIVES

Before you start writing objectives it might help to know what they look like. Here are some examples:

- Know the basic terminology of the subject (a general objective).
- Understand the changing relationship between money income and real income as prices change (Economics).
- Derive pressure drop and heat-transfer relations for flow in smooth pipes (Engineering).
- Obtain a problem-oriented history from a patient (Medicine).
- Develop a scholarly concern for accuracy (general attitudinal objective).
- Defend one's judgements against the informed criticism of peers (English).

In each case, the objective contains a statement which suggests the kind of behaviour that students will be required to demonstrate in order to show that the objective has been achieved. Now, if you look at each objective again, you will notice that they suggest rather different kinds of behaviour. The first three objectives require information of an intellectual kind for their achievement and may be classified as **knowledge objectives**. The fourth objective refers to a skill of a practical kind and is thus described as a **skill objective**. The fifth objective suggests an attitude of mind and is therefore classified as an **attitudinal objective**. The last objective demands a knowledge background, as well as the skills of intellectual debate and argument.

The three broad divisions – knowledge, skills and attitudes – are often used in grouping objectives but you may come across several refinements of each division in the literature. The most common of these refinements is the taxonomy developed by Bloom and his colleagues. They call the three divisions 'domains': cognitive (knowledge and intellectual skills), psychomotor (physical skills) and affective (feelings and attitudes).

These domains have been subdivided to provide hierarchies of objectives of increasing complexity.

Knowledge objectives (the cognitive domain): It is in this area that Bloom's taxonomy has been most widely applied. He proposes six levels – knowledge, comprehension, application, analysis, synthesis and evaluation. Though these provide an intellectual framework for preparing objectives, for everyday use, you may find it more practical to 'collapse' them into three subdivisions:

- Recall of information
- Understanding
- Problem-solving

The reason for keeping different levels in mind when writing objectives is that courses sometimes pay undue attention to one level (usually the recall of information).

Skill objectives (the psychomotor domain): Bloom and his colleagues did not develop a hierarchy of objectives in the psychomotor domain, though others have attempted to do so. In many courses, teachers need to pay a great deal of attention to developing skill objectives. Such objectives may be improved if the condition under which the performance is to occur, and the criteria of acceptable performance, can be indicated.

One way you might find useful is to specify competent performance using the hierarchy developed by Korst. He suggests that there will be some skills with which one would expect students to show a high degree of competence and others with which one might only expect familiarity. His hierarchy is: well-qualified or very competent; familiar with or competent; awareness or minimal familiarity.

Attitudinal objectives (the affective domain): Writing objectives in the affective area is very difficult, which possibly explains why they are so often ignored. This is unfortunate because, implicitly or explicitly, there are many attitudinal qualities we hope to see in our graduating students. As Krathwohl has a taxonomy in this domain you could approach the task in much the same way as writing knowledge objectives.

Another way is to attempt to define the starting attitudes of the students and match these with more desirable attitudes towards which you would hope they would move. For example, you could be concerned with the attitude of students to something. You might start by assuming that the students had a stereotyped attitude. You would then wish to move them away from this towards an attitude which demonstrated understanding and acceptance of other views. The advantage of this method is that it recognizes that not all students will develop the desired attitude nor will they all necessarily start a course with the same attitudes. The way to express objectives using this approach is to state 'Away from ... (a particular attitude), towards ... (a desirable attitude)'.

Where do objectives come from?

Writing objectives is not simply a process of sitting, pen in hand, waiting for inspiration, although original thinking is certainly encouraged. Objectives will come from a careful consideration of the subject matter, what you and your colleagues know about students, and about the subject. This will not be an easy task. You should consider a wide range of sources for objectives. These include:

- an analysis of your own and colleagues' knowledge, skills and attitudes;
- ways of thinking and problem-solving to be developed;
- students' interests, needs and characteristics;
- subject matter, as reflected in the published literature (especially in suitable textbooks);
- the needs of society;
- the requirements of professional certifying authorities;
- the objectives of the department or faculty.

How specific and detailed should objectives be?

This is a question frequently asked. The answer depends on the purposes for which the objectives are to be used. In designing a course, the objectives will be more general than the objectives for a particular teaching session within the course. As objective writing can become tedious, trivial and time-consuming it is best to keep your objectives simple, unambiguous and broad enough to convey clearly your intentions. To illustrate from our own field of teaching, the objectives for a six-week clinical skills course, conducted for groups of 9–10 fifth-year students, is shown below. Though quite broad, these objectives have proved detailed enough for course planning purposes and for making the intentions of the programme clear to students.

FIGURE 5.2

EXAMPLE OF COURSE OBJECTIVES

OBJECTIVES	TEACHING AND LEARNING ACTIVITIES	ASSESSMENTS
AT THE COMPLETION OF THE COURSE THE STUDENT WILL BE ABLE TO		
1 TAKE A COMPREHENSIVE HISTORY	1	1
2 PERFORM A COMPLETE PHYSICAL EXAMINATION	2	2
3 WRITE UP THE HISTORY AND EXAMINATION AND CONSTRUCT A PROBLEM LIST	3	3
4 MAKE DECISIONS ON DIAGNOSIS, INVESTIGATION AND MANAGEMENT	4	4
5 RELATE WELL TO PATIENTS	5	5
6 SHOW THAT HE/SHE HAS IMPROVED HIS/HER KNOWLEDGE OF MEDICINE AND SURGERY	6	6

CHOOSING METHODS AND RELATING OBJECTIVES TO TEACHING AND LEARNING ACTIVITIES

The methods you employ to achieve the objectives should not only allow those objectives to be realized, but will also reflect the kind of orientation you have to curriculum development. If your orientation is primarily the transmission of content, it is likely that your teaching methods will be dominated by lectures, assigned reading and set problem-solving exercises; if it is to the intellectual and personal development of your students, small group teaching or individual tutorials are likely to play a more important role.

The actual choice of methods will be governed by several factors. Among the most important will be:

- your own expertise in using different methods;
- your willingness to experiment;
- resources to support the method you wish to use;
- student level and ability.

Before leaving this subject we should like you to consider one important matter about choice of methods. Courses are often constructed in ways that reveal a growing complexity of subject matter. For example, early in the first year there may be an emphasis on basic principles and ideas. In later years, subject matter may be very much more complex and demanding. Yet, in our experience, the teaching methods used in the later years do not generally demand higher levels of intellectual performance and personal involvement.

The main types of teaching undertaken in higher education, such as lecturing, small group teaching and practical teaching, are dealt with in earlier chapters. These are by no means all of the methods available. Other possibilities include field-work, peer teaching and a variety of simulation techniques. In addition, it should be remembered that students undertake many learning activities in the absence of teaching. This should be kept in mind with due allowances being made for independent learning. It is not unreasonable to make explicit in your objectives, areas where you expect the students to work on their own. This particularly applies to knowledge objectives which might be achieved just as well independently as by a series of didactic lectures. It could also apply to some skill objectives where students might be expected to seek out relevant experience by themselves.

The way in which this process has been followed through in the clinical skills course we have already introduced is

FIGURE 5·3
EXAMPLE OF MATCHING TEACHING AND LEARNING ACTIVITIES TO COURSE OBJECTIVES

OBJECTIVES	TEACHING AND LEARNING ACTIVITIES	ASSESSMENTS
AT THE COMPLETION OF THE COURSE THE STUDENT WILL BE ABLE TO 1 TAKE A COMPREHENSIVE HISTORY	1 PRECEPTOR SESSIONS WITH REVIEW OF VIDEO RECORDINGS OF PATIENT INTERVIEWS	
2 PERFORM A COMPLETE PHYSICAL EXAMINATION	2 VIEWING DEMONSTRATION VIDEOTAPE. PRECEPTOR SESSIONS WITH PATIENTS. WARD PRACTICE. WARD ROUNDS WITH RESIDENT STAFF	
3 WRITE UP THE HISTORY AND EXAMINATION AND CONSTRUCT A PROBLEM LIST	3 TAPE-SLIDE PROGRAMME ON PROBLEM-ORIENTED RECORD KEEPING. WRITE-UPS ON WARD PATIENTS. PRECEPTOR SESSIONS TO CHECK AND DISCUSS WRITE-UPS.	
4 MAKE DECISIONS ON DIAGNOSIS, INVESTIGATIONS AND MANAGEMENT	4 PROBLEM-BASED WHOLE GROUP DISCUSSION SESSIONS. REVIEW OF CASE WRITE-UPS.	
5 RELATE WELL TO PATIENTS	5 PRECEPTOR SESSIONS WITH REVIEW OF VIDEO RECORDINGS OF PATIENT INTERVIEWS.	
6 SHOW THAT HE/SHE HAS IMPROVED HIS/HER KNOWLEDGE OF MEDICINE AND SURGERY	6 INDEPENDENT LEARNING. PREPARATION OF CASES FOR PRESENTATION. TAPE-SLIDE TUTORIALS. COMPUTERIZED SELF-ASSESSMENT PROGRAMMES.	

demonstrated once again on the course planning chart (Figure 5.3). When planning this course we were aware that many students were deficient in their basic history-taking and physical examination skills. We thus decided to put the majority of our staff time into achieving the first two objectives. The most appropriate teaching method was obviously direct observation with feedback and as this is very time-consuming we opted for a preceptor system where one staff member was responsible for only three students throughout the programme. However, opportunity was also provided for students to obtain additional ward practice on their own and the resident staff were also mobilized to provide further help and instruction in this area. One of the implications of this decision on staff allocation was to accept that the sixth objective (improving their knowledge in the subjects Medicine and Surgery) would have to be achieved by other methods. This has involved an expectation that students accept responsibility for doing much of this themselves. We have also designed and prepared a variety of self-instructional materials. Other teaching techniques are incorporated to achieve other objectives.

RELATING OBJECTIVES TO ASSESSMENT METHODS

Just as it is important to match the teaching and learning methods with the objectives, it is important to match the assessment methods to the objectives. Failure to do so is an important reason why courses fail to live up to expectations. A mismatch of assessment and objectives may lead to serious distortions of student learning (see also Chapters 6 and 8).

In designing your course, we believe that it is important to distinguish carefully between two types of assessment. One is primarily designed to give feedback to the students as they go along (**formative assessment**). The other is to assess their abilities for the purposes of grading (**summative assessment**). Formative assessment is a crucial part of the educational process, especially where complex intellectual and practical skills are to be mastered. Such assessment is notoriously deficient in many courses in higher education.

FIGURE 5.4
EXAMPLE OF MATCHING ASSESSMENT PROCEDURES TO COURSE OBJECTIVES

The way in which assessment was designed in the example of our clinical skills course is shown in Figure 5.4. As no formal examination is required at the completion of the course, the

OBJECTIVES	TEACHING AND LEARNING ACTIVITIES	ASSESSMENTS
AT THE COMPLETION OF THE COURSE THE STUDENT WILL BE ABLE TO **1** TAKE A COMPREHENSIVE HISTORY	**1** PRECEPTOR SESSIONS WITH REVIEW OF VIDEO RECORDINGS OF PATIENT INTERVIEWS.	**1** ASSESSMENT OF VIDEO RECORDING DURING COURSE (FORMATIVE). ASSESSMENT OF VIDEO RECORDING AT END OF COURSE (SUMMATIVE).
2 PERFORM A COMPLETE PHYSICAL EXAMINATION	**2** VIEWING DEMONSTRATION VIDEO TAPE. PRECEPTOR SESSIONS WITH PATIENTS. WARD PRACTICE. WARD ROUNDS WITH RESIDENT STAFF.	**2** DIRECT OBSERVATION DURING COURSE (FORMATIVE). DIRECT OBSERVATION AT END OF COURSE (SUMMATIVE).
3 WRITE UP THE HISTORY AND EXAMINATION AND CONSTRUCT A PROBLEM LIST	**3** TAPE-SLIDE PROGRAMME ON PROBLEM ORIENTATED RECORD KEEPING. WRITE-UPS ON WARD PATIENTS. PRECEPTOR SESSIONS TO CHECK AND DISCUSS WRITE-UPS.	**3** MARKING AND DISCUSSION OF CASE WRITE-UPS DURING COURSE (FORMATIVE). MARKING OF CASE WRITE-UPS AT END OF COURSE (SUMMATIVE).
4 MAKE DECISIONS ON DIAGNOSIS INVESTIGATION AND MANAGEMENT	**4** PROBLEM-BASED WHOLE GROUP DISCUSSION SESSIONS. REVIEW OF CASE WRITE-UPS.	**4** PERFORMANCE IN WHOLE GROUP SESSIONS (SUMMATIVE).
5 RELATE WELL TO PATIENTS	**5** PRECEPTOR SESSIONS WITH REVIEW OF VIDEO-RECORDINGS OF PATIENT INTERVIEWS.	**5** ASSESSMENT OF VIDEO RECORDINGS DURING COURSE (FORMATIVE AND SUMMATIVE).
6 SHOW THAT HE/SHE HAS IMPROVED HIS/HER KNOWLEDGE OF MEDICINE AND SURGERY	**6** INDEPENDENT LEARNING. PREPARATION OF CASES FOR PRESENTATION. TAPE/SLIDE TUTORIALS. COMPUTERIZED SELF-ASSESSMENT PROGRAMMES.	**6** SELF-ASSESSMENT. COMPUTERIZED SELF-ASSESSMENT PROGRAMMES (FORMATIVE)

major emphasis of the assessment activities is formative. However, assessment activities of a summative type are conducted during the final two weeks of the programme when aspects of the student's performance are observed by preceptors and by other staff members. You will note that the assessment of knowledge is left largely to the students themselves. In other circumstances we might have used a written test to assess this component of the course.

SEQUENCING AND ORGANIZING THE COURSE

It is unlikely that the way in which you have set out your objectives, teaching and assessment on the planning chart will be the best chronological or practical way to present the course to students. There are several things that must be done. First, there must be a **grouping** of related objectives and activities. (In the example we are following throughout this chapter, such a grouping occurs for objectives one to three which are largely to be achieved by the preceptor sessions.) Secondly, there must be a **sequencing** of the teaching activities. There are likely to be circumstances in your own context that influence you to sequence a course in a particular way, such as semesters or teaching terms. However, there are also a number of educational grounds upon which to base the sequencing. These include:

- proceeding from what students know to what they do not know;
- proceeding from concrete experiences to abstract reasoning;
- the logical or historical development of a subject;
- important themes or concepts;
- starting from unusual, novel or complex situations and working backwards towards understanding.

OTHER COURSE DESIGN CONSIDERATIONS

Many of the important educational considerations in designing a course have been addressed, but there are other matters that must be dealt with before a course can be mounted. These are only briefly described because the way in which they are handled depends very much on the administrative arrangements of the particular situation in which you teach. Having said that, we are not suggesting in any way that your educational plans must be subservient to administrative considerations. Clearly, in the best of all possible worlds, the administrative considerations would be entirely subservient to the educational plans but the reality is that there will be a series of trade-offs, with educational considerations hopefully paramount.

In planning your new course, you will need to take the following into account.

Administrative responsibilities: It will be necessary for one person to assume the responsibility of course co-ordination. This job will require the scheduling of teachers, students, teaching activities, assessment time and resources.

Allocation of time: Many courses are over-ambitious and require far more time (often on the part of students) for their completion than is reasonable. This is especially true of parts of a larger course of study. In allocating time, you will need to consider the total time available and its breakdown, and how time is to be spent in the course. It is often desirable to use blocks of time to deal with a particular topic, rather than 'spinning it out' over a term, semester or year.

Allocation of teaching rooms, laboratories and equipment: Courses depend for their success on the careful allocation of resources. Allocative procedures vary, but it is important that all competing claims are settled early so that orderly teaching can take place.

Technical and administrative support: Whether you teach a course alone, or as one of a team, you will find a need for support of some kind or other. It may be as simple as the services of a typist to prepare course notes and examination papers, or as complex as requiring, at different times, the assistance of audiovisual technicians, laboratory staff and computer programmers. Your needs for support must be considered at the planning stage.

EVALUATING THE COURSE

Many teachers may find a discussion of course evaluation in a chapter on planning rather odd, perhaps believing that this activity is something that takes place **after** a course has been completed. We believe that this generally should not be the case. It is our contention that in teaching you should be progressively evaluating what you are doing and how the course design and plans are working out in practice. In this way, modifications and adjustments can be made in a planned and informed manner. But what is evaluation? You will often find the terms 'evaluation' and 'assessment' used interchangeably, but evaluation is generally understood to refer to the process of obtaining information about a course (or teaching) for subsequent judgement and decision-making. This process, properly done, will involve you in rather more than handing around a student questionnaire during the last lecture. What you do clearly depends on what you want to find out, but thorough course planning and course revision will require information about three different aspects of your course. These are the context of and inputs into your course, the processes of teaching, learning, assessment and course administration and, finally, the outcomes of the course.

Context and input evaluation: This is crucial if mistakes and problems are not to be attributed, unfairly, to teachers. In this type of evaluation you will need to consider the course in relation to such matters as other related courses, the entering abilities and characteristics of students, the resources and equipment available to teach with, and the overall design and planning arrangements for the course. The major sources of information you can use here will be in the form of course documents, student records, financial statements and the like.

Process evaluation: This focuses on the conduct of the teaching, learning, assessment and administration. It is here that the views of students can be sought as they are the only people who experience the full impact of teaching in the course. Questionnaires, written statements, interviews and discussion are techniques that you can consider.

Outcome evaluation: This looks at student attainments at the end of the course. Naturally you will review the results of assessment and judge whether they meet with the implied and expressed hopes for the course. Discussion with students and observation of aspects of their behaviour will help you determine their attitudes to the course you have taught.

In all evaluations, whether of a course or of teaching, it is helpful to keep in mind that there are many sources of information available to you and a variety of methods you can use (Figure 5.5).

FIGURE 5.5
COURSE/TEACHING EVALUATION

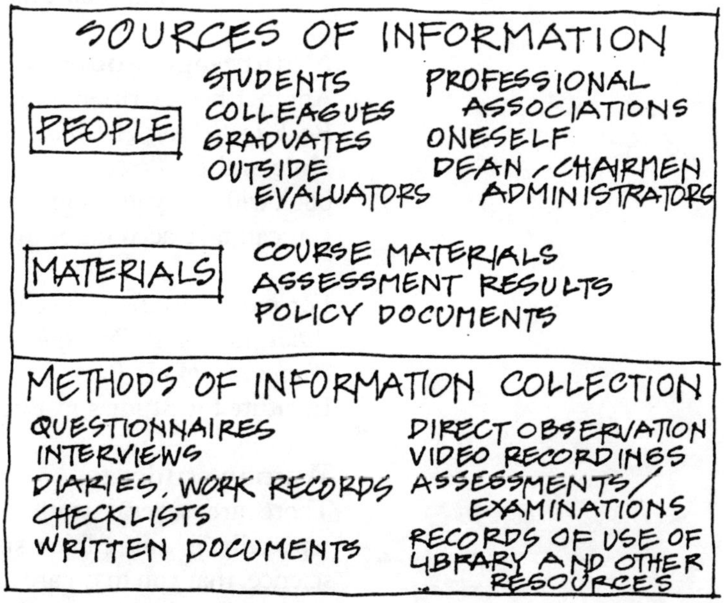

The literature on evaluation will guide you on using these diverse sources and methods. We recommend the references to Roe and his colleagues (1983, 1986) in the knowledge that they contain many helpful practical examples of checklists, interview schedules and questionnaires. You may also wish to refer to the course evaluation questionnaire at the end of Chapter 1.

GUIDED READING

For a useful extension of the material in this chapter we suggest you have a look at the appropriate sections in Beard and Hartley's book *Teaching and Learning in Higher Education*, Harper & Row, London, 1984; including their consideration of different groups of students.

More specific discussions of student matters include the following recommended sources:

Overseas students
Although written for students, you will undoubtedly profit from a reading of Brigid Ballard and John Clanchy's book *Study Abroad, A Manual for Asian Students*, Longman Malaysia, Kuala Lumpur, 1984. Obviously, you might also recommend this to your students and possibly even use some of the material in it as a basis for tutorial discussion.

Mature-age students
Another book written for students that you will find helpful is *Back to School: A Guide for Adults Returning to Study* by T Hore and L West, Methuen, North Ryde NSW, 1982. This book will give you insights into the students' perspective which you can take account of in your teaching and planning.

For more specific advice on curriculum planning we suggest *Adult Learning Principles and their Application to Program Planning* by D H Brundage and D MacKeracher, The Ontario Institute for Studies in Education, Toronto, 1980.

Women students
There are several studies and guides concerning women, especially in disciplines such as mathematics and physical science, that you may care to follow-up. A more general source is that edited by Nancy J Evans, *Facilitating the Development of Women*. This book is number 29 in the New Directions for Student Services series published by Jossey-Bass, San Francisco, in 1985. Chapters in this book address diverse concerns, including those of young undergraduate women, minorities and older women in higher education.

First-year students
Here all of the references to student learning given in Chapter 8 are relevant and recommended for use in planning for first-year teaching. A W Astin, *Preventing Students from Dropping Out*, Jossey-Bass, San Francisco, 1975, is also helpful.

If you are keen to look at **course planning** in depth, you could obtain a copy of the book by D Dallas *et al* entitled *Studies in Course Design*, Vol 1, University Teaching Methods Unit (now the Centre for Staff Development in Higher Education), University of London, 1978.

Another helpful textbook on course planning has been written by William H Berquist, *et al*. Entitled *Designing Undergraduate Education*, it examines the following six curricular dimensions; time, space, resources, organization, procedures and outcomes. Ths book was published by Jossey-Bass, San Francisco, in 1981.

The literature on **objectives** is very extensive. A useful guide is the book by R Beard, F G Healey and P J Holloway called *Objectives in Higher Education* (2nd Edn), Society for Research in Higher Education, London, 1974.

The self-instructional book by R Mager, *Preparing Instructional Objectives* (2nd Edn), Lake, Belmont, California, 1984 is a useful how-to-do-it guide by the best-known advocate of the use of objectives in teaching.

There are numerous books on **teaching methods** available and we suggest you browse in your institution's library for suitable material. Some recent titles we can recommend are *Teaching Thinking by Discussion* edited by Donald Bligh, SRHE/NFER-Nelson, Guildford, UK, 1986; *Problem-Based Learning in Education for the Professions* edited by David Boud, Higher Education Research and Development Society of Australasia, Sydney, 1985; and *Synergogy: A New Strategy for Education, Training and Development* by J S Mouton and R R Blake, Jossey-Bass, San Francisco, 1984. ('Synergogy' is a term coined by these writers to describe a method in which the members of small teams learn from one another. Higher education examples of the method are provided for illustration.)

Finally, we suggest *Reflection: Turning Experience into Learning* edited by D Boud, R Keogh and D Walker, Kogan Page/ Nichols, New York, 1985; especially for those in postgraduate professional education and adult education.

For a thorough discussion of **evaluation**, plus examples of evaluation methods (eg questionnaires), we suggest you obtain copies of: E Roe and R McDonald, *Informed Professional Judgement: A Guide to Evaluation in Post-Secondary Education*, University of Queensland Press, Brisbane, 1983; and E Roe, R McDonald and I Moses, *Reviewing Academic Performance*, University of Queensland Press, Brisbane, 1986.

Books referred to in this chapter:

Taxonomy of Educational Objectives. Handbook I: Cognitive Domain by B S Bloom *et al*, McKay, New York, 1956.

Taxonomy of Educational Objectives. Handbook II: Affective Domain by D R Krathwohl, B S Bloom and B B Masia, McKay, New York, 1962.

A Guide to the Clinical Clerkship in Medicine by D R Korst, University of Wisconsin, 1973.

Curriculum Perspectives and Practice by J P Miller and W Seller, Longman, New York, 1985.

Chapter 6 Assessing the Students

INTRODUCTION

Being involved in student assessment is perhaps the most critical of all tasks facing the teacher. Generally, teachers take such involvement quite seriously but, sadly, the quality of many assessment and examination procedures leaves much to be desired. The aim of this chapter, therefore, will be to help you to ensure that the assessments with which you are involved will measure what they are supposed to measure in as fair and as accurate a way as possible. We will provide some background information about the purposes of assessment and the basic principles of education measurement. We will then detail the forms of assessment with which you should be familiar in order that you can select an appropriate method.

THE PURPOSE OF ASSESSMENT

When faced with developing an assessment you must be quite clear about its purpose. This may appear to be stating the obvious but try asking your colleagues what they think is the purpose of the assessment with which you are concerned. We are certain that there will be a considerable diversity of opinion. Some may see it as testing the students' mastery of the course content, others may see it as a way of ranking the students, and yet others as a way of encouraging students to study the course *vis-à-vis* another concurrent course.

Mehrens and Lehmann identify several purposes of assessment which may be paraphrased as follows:

- Judging mastery of essential skills and knowledge
- Measuring improvement over time
- Diagnosing student difficulties
- Evaluating the teaching methods

- Evaluating the effectiveness of the course
- Motivating students to study

Though it may be possible for one assessment method to achieve more than one of these purposes, all too often assessments are used for inappropriate purposes and consequently fail to provide valid and reliable data.

It must never be forgotten how powerfully an assessment affects students, particularly if it is one on which their future may depend. This influence may be positive or negative and even harmful. For many students, passing the examination at the end of the course is their primary motivation. Should this examination not be valid, and thus not truly reflect the content and objectives of the course, then the potential for serious distortions in learning and for making errors of judgement about students is evident. An example from our own experience may illustrate this point. A revision of the final-year medical curriculum inadvertently led to the multiple-choice test component of the end-of-year assessment having considerably more weight than the clinical component. Students were observed to be spending excessive amounts of time studying the theoretical aspects of the course in preference to practising their clinical skills, the latter being the main aim of the curriculum revision. A subsequent modification of the assessment scheme, giving equal weighting to an assessment of clinical competence, has corrected this unsatisfactory state of affairs.

It is our view that assessments on which decisions about the students' future are to be made (summative assessment) should be kept separate from assessments which are for the benefit of the students in terms of guiding their further study (formative assessment).

Summative assessment

In dealing with summative assessment, every effort must be made to ensure that all assessments are fair and based on appropriate criteria. Students should be fully informed of these criteria, on the assessment methods to be employed and on the weightings to be given to each component. Such information should be given to students when a course begins. This is important because it is surprising how often information obtained from other sources, such as past students or even from the department itself, can be inaccurate, misleading or misinterpreted by the students. The best way of avoiding this is to provide printed details of the course plan, including the assessment scheme. Examples of past papers can be provided and we have found an open forum on the assessment scheme early in the course to be both popular and valuable.

Formative assessment

Formative assessments can be organized more informally. Such assessments must be free of threat, as the aim is to get the students to reveal their strengths and weaknesses rather than to disguise them. Opportunities to obtain feedback on knowledge or performance are always appreciated by students and can lead to positive feelings about the department and the staff concerned.

WHAT YOU SHOULD KNOW ABOUT EDUCATIONAL MEASUREMENT

Whatever the purpose of the assessment, the method used should satisfy the following three requirements:

1 **Validity:** Does it measure what it is supposed to measure?
2 **Reliability:** Does it produce consistent results?
3 **Practicality:** Is it practical in terms of time and resources?

Our intention in raising these requirements is to encourage you to apply the same critical interest in the quality of educational assessment as you undoubtedly appy to the quality of your research. This section will provide you with some basic information about aspects of educational measurement with which we think you should be familiar.

Validity

Content validity is the first priority of any assessment. It is a measure of the degree to which the assessment contains a representative sample of the material taught in the course. A numerical value cannot be placed against it and it must be judged according to the objectives of the assessment. Therefore, in approaching any assessment the first question you must ask is: **what are the objectives of the course**?

Unfortunately, such objectives are not always available. Should you be in this situation, with no written objectives for the assessment you have to design, then you have no alternative but to develop them. This is not such a difficult task as you might imagine because, as far as the assessment is concerned, the objectives are embodied in the course content. A look at the teaching programme, lecture and tutorial topics, and discussions with teaching staff should allow you to identify and categorize the key features of the course. What you are, in fact, attempting to do is to construct a course plan in reverse and you may find it helpful at this point to consult Chapter 5 on curriculum planning where this process is discussed in greater detail.

The objectives of the course, however categorized, are the framework against which you can evaluate the content validity. For the content validity to be high, the assessment must sample the students' abilities **on each objective**. As these objectives are likely to cover a wide range of knowledge, skills and attitudes, it will immediately become apparent that no single test method is likely to provide a valid assessment. For instance, an essay test will hardly be likely to provide valid information about practical laboratory skills.

Other forms of validity exist but generally speaking you will not be in a position to evaluate them so they will not be discussed further. If you are interested, you should consult the guided reading at the end of the chapter.

Reliability

The realiability of any assessment is a measure of the consistency and precision with which it tests what it is supposed to test. Though its importance is initially less vital than validity, you should remember that an unreliable assessment cannot be valid. The degree of reliability varies with the test format itself, the quality of its administration and the marking.

Theoretically, a reliable test should produce the same result if administered to the same student on two separate occasions. The statistic describing the degree to which this happens is called the 'coefficient of stability'. In most situations, practical considerations make it impossible to provide such information. This difficulty is normally overcome by providing a measure of **internal consistency**.

The basic principle of this statistical technique is to split the test into two parts and assume that these parts are equivalent. A test with a high degree of internal consistency shows a high correlation between the student's performance in each half of the test. The most commonly used statistics of this type are the Kuder–Richardson formulas. You will frequently come across these formulas in computer-scored multiple-choice tests.

The other key component in determining the reliability of a test is the **consistency of the marking**. The absence of consistency is responsible for the unacceptable levels of reliability in most forms of direct assessment and of written tests of the essay type. However, methods are available to help you minimize this problem and these will be discussed later in this chapter.

Improving validity and reliability of tests

Validity can be improved by:

- carefully matching a test with the course objectives, content and teaching methods;
- increasing the sample of objectives and content areas included in any given test;
- using test methods that are appropriate for the objectives specified;
- employing a range of test methods;
- ensuring adequate security and supervision to avoid cheating;
- improving the reliability of the test.

Reliability can be improved by:

- ensuring that questions are clear and suitable for the level of the students;
- checking to make sure test time limits are realistic;
- writing test instructions that are simple, clear, and unambiguous;
- developing a marking scheme of high quality (eg explicit and agreed criteria, checking of marks, several skilled markers);
- keeping choices within a test paper to a minimum;
- when using less reliable test methods increasing the number of questions, observations or examination time.

Practicality

An assessment scheme must be feasible. You may decide to use a scheme that is potentially highly valid and reliable but find that it is not practical to do so in your circumstances. Some questions you might consider here are:

- Do I have the skills to administer, mark and grade the assessment?
- Can I interpret the results accurately?
- Will the assessment scheme demand too much time?
- Does the scheme require special resources (eg labour, materials or equipment) and are these readily available to me?

Obviously, there will be other considerations of a practical nature that are peculiar to your own circumstances and that you will have to consider before implementing any particular scheme.

Norm-referenced versus criterion-referenced assessment

Before we finish dealing with some of the basic principles of educational measurement, we wish to be satisfied that you understand the difference between norm- and criterion-

referenced assessment. You are likely to be familiar with norm-referenced assessment, as this reflects the traditional approach to testing. Any assessment which uses the results of all the students to determine the standard is of this type. In such tests the pass level is often determined arbitrarily, by predetermining the proportion of students given each grade, or statistically, by using the standard deviation.

In professional fields it is necessary that the students achieve some minimal standard of competence. If this is the main purpose of the assessment then the criterion-referenced approach is more appropriate. Such an approach necessitates the determination of the standard before administering the examination, rather than waiting to see the overall results before doing so. Though this is difficult to implement, and even then often has to be modified for practical reasons (eg too many students would fail), we have found that attempting to do so is a powerful way of improving the validity of the assessment. Everyone concerned is forced to consider each item in the examination and ask themselves if it is relevant and set at the appropriate level of difficulty. Our own experiences with such an examination used to test clinical competence in the final year of the medical degree have been very revealing and rewarding.

ASSESSMENT METHODS

In planning your assessment, it is necessary to be aware of the variety of methods available to you. It is impossible to be comprehensive for reasons of space so we will restrict ourselves to some common methods. We will also include information about some innovative approaches developed recently which may be of interest. We do this deliberately in an attempt to encourage you to become subversive! With your new-found knowledge of assessment you will soon be involved in situations where it is obvious that inappropriate methods are being used. This may be due to a combination of tradition, ignorance and prejudice. The first two you may be able to influence by rational argument based on the type of information we provide in this book. The last is a more difficult problem with which to deal.

TYPES OF ASSESSMENT

1. Essay
2. Short-answer
3. Objective (multiple-choice, true–false)
4. Direct observation
5. Oral
6. Structured practical assessment
7. Self-assessment

1. ESSAY

We suggest caution in the use of the essay, except in situations where its unique attributes are required. The essay is the only means we have to assess students' ability to compose an answer and present it in effective prose. It can also indirectly measure attitudes, values and opinions. There are other reasons for the continuing popularity of essays. Of particular importance in higher education seem to be the assumptions that the production of language and verbalization of thought is a scholarly activity of considerable worth and that essays encourage students to develop more desirable study habits.

Though they are relatively easy to set, essays are time-consuming to mark. The widespread use of multiple-choice tests and the advent of computer-scoring has lifted the marking burden from many academics, few of whom would wish to take it up again. Excluding such selfish reasons, there are other grounds for caution with essays. The most important is the potential for unreliable marking. Several studies have shown significant differences between the marks allocated by different examiners and even by the same examiner re-marking the same papers at a later date.

Essay questions tend to be of two kinds. The first is the **extended response**. An example is seen in Figure 6.1.

In the extended response question the student's factual knowledge and ability to provide and organize ideas, to substantiate them and to present them in coherent English are

FIGURE 6.1
EXAMPLE OF EXTENDED RESPONSE ESSAY QUESTION

> COMPARE AND CONTRAST ESSAY TESTS WITH OBJECTIVE TESTS IN HIGHER EDUCATION.

tested. The extended essay is useful for testing knowledge objectives at the higher levels.

Another type of essay question is the **restricted response,** an example of which is shown in Figure 6.2. The restricted response form sets explicit boundaries on the answer required and on its organization.

FIGURE 6.2
EXAMPLE OF RESTRICTED RESPONSE ESSAY QUESTION

> EXPLAIN THE ADVANTAGES AND DISADVANTAGES OF ESSAY TESTS AND OBJECTIVE TESTS IN HIGHER EDUCATION WITH REFERENCE TO:
> 1. VALIDITY
> 2. RELIABILITY AND
> 3. PRACTICALITY

This type of essay is best used for testing lower-level knowledge objectives. An advantage of the more restricted format is that it can decrease the scoring problems (and hence be more reliable).

Essays can be constructed in ways that – in theory at least – can test different levels of intellectual processes. Three simple examples are given:

Recall of basic principles

DESCRIBE THE THREE BASIC REQUIREMENTS THAT MUST BE MET BY AN ASSESSMENT METHOD.

Analysis

WHY IS THERE SO MUCH DISSATISFACTION WITH EXAMINATIONS?

Evaluation

"WE CANNOT HAVE REAL LEARNING IN SCHOOL IF WE THINK IT IS OUR DUTY AND RIGHT TO TELL CHILDREN WHAT THEY MUST LEARN." (JOHN HOLT). EITHER CRITICIZE OR DEFEND THIS STATEMENT.

There are numerous models of essay questions and illustrations of how they can be constructed to test for different objectives. We suggest you have a look at the book by Bloom, Hastings and Madaus for assistance with this.

If you intend to set and mark essay questions in an examination, then we suggest that you keep in mind the points in Figure 6.3.

FIGURE 6.3
PROCEDURE FOR SETTING AND MARKING ESSAY QUESTIONS

Procedure

A Write questions that elicit the type of response suggested by the objectives.

Use clear directive words such as 'describe', 'compare', 'contrast', 'criticize' and 'explain'. If 'discuss' is used, be sure to indicate what points should be discussed.

Establish a clear framework which aims the student to the desired response. Rather than: 'Discuss small group teaching' try 'Describe the educational benefits to be derived by including a programme of small group teaching in a course of study'.

B Set more questions requiring shorter answers of about a page, rather than a few questions requiring long answers.

This will provide a better sampling of course content, will reduce bias in marking for quantity rather than quality, and will improve reliability.

C Ensure that all students are required to answer the same or equivalent questions.

Constructing optional questions of equal difficulty is hard and, further, you will not be able to make valid comparisons among students if they have answered questions that are not equivalent.

D Prepare a marking system.

Two methods are commonly used, both of which require you to prepare a model answer. In the **analytical method** of marking, a checklist of specific points is prepared against which marks are allocated. Such factors as 'logical argument' or 'expression' should be included if you think they are relevant. If you wish to reward legibility and presentation, give these components a proportion of the marks but avoid these aspects unduly biasing your assessment of the content. The **global method** of marking can be used if you have at least 30 papers to mark. Papers are read rapidly and assigned to one of five or more piles, grading from a superior response down to the inferior. Papers are then re-read to check the original sorting. This is a faster and more reliable method of marking once standards for the various piles have been established.

E Mark questions with the following points in mind:

Mark anonymously.
Mark only one question at a time or, preferably, have a separate marker for each question.
Adopt consistent standards.
Try to mark each question without interruption.
Preferably have two independent markers for each question and average the result, or at least re-read a sample of papers to check marking consistency.

For essays, or other written assignments required during a course of study, you can also take steps to improve the quality of feedback to students. One way is to use an assignment attachment of the kind shown in Figure 6.4, remembering that this particular form was designed for a specific course and should be adapted for your own specific needs.

Not only can this attachment provide very useful individual feedback, but used early in a course with a model answer, it can show students the standards you expect from them, and also help you in awarding marks.

2. SHORT-ANSWER AND SIMPLE COMPUTATION QUESTIONS

Short-answer tests have been surprisingly little used in recent years, yet another casualty of the multiple-choice boom.

FIGURE 6·4 AN ASSIGNMENT ATTACHMENT

energy and life systems

ASSIGNMENT ATTACHMENT

Prepared with the assistance of Educational Services & Teaching Resources Unit Murdoch University

Student's name: Assignment grade:

	Itemised Rating Scale (ticked *when applicable*) ←— —→				
STRUCTURE					
Essay relevant to topic					Essay has little relevance
Topic covered in depth					Superficial treatment of topic
ARGUMENT					
Accurate presentation of evidence					Much evidence inaccurate or questionable
Logically developed argument					Essay rambles & lacks continuity
Original & creative thought					Little evidence of originality
STYLE					
Fluent piece of writing					Clumsily written
Succinct writing					Unnecessarily repetitive
PRESENTATION					
Legible & well set out work					Untidy & difficult to read
Reasonable length					Over/under length
SOURCES					
Adequate acknowledgement of sources					Inadequate acknowledgement of sources
Correct citation of references					Incorrect referencing
MECHANICS					
Grammatical sentences					Several ungrammatical sentences
Correct spelling throughout					Much incorrect spelling
Effective use of figures & tables					Figures & tables add little to argument
Correct use of units & quantities					Some units incorrect

Please turn over

NOTES

- Sections left blank are not relevant to this assignment

- Some aspects are more important than others, so there is no formula connecting the number of ticks in different boxes with the grade.

- Key to grades:

  A An outstanding piece of work

  B Very good

  C Satisfactory

  D Generally unsatisfactory

  F Inadequate in most respects

- A tick in the left-hand box means that the statement on the left is true: a tick in the second box from the left means that the statement on the left is true to some extent. Similarly for the right-hand boxes. e.g.

  Topic covered in depth [ ] [ ] [✓] [ ] Superficial treatment of topic

  means that the topic was treated somewhat superficially in the assignment.

- Ticks in the right hand boxes show areas of deficiency in the report.

EXPLANATION AND COMMENTS:

____

Tutor

Though easy to mark, it is essential that markers are provided with a well-constructed marking key, especially if more than one correct answer is possible, or if several processes are involved in answering the question. (See Figure 6.5.)

FIGURE 6·5
EXAMPLE OF A SIMPLE SHORT-ANSWER QUESTION WITH ANSWER KEY

HOW MANY CONSONANTS ARE THERE IN THE WORD AUSTRALIA?

ANSWER: 4 (ONE MARK)

Clarifying the marking key is critical. In a very simple exercise that we conduct in our assessment workshops, we find that a group of markers will invariably give the piece of work shown in Figure 6.6 a mark ranging from 0 to 10 out of a maximum of 10!

FIGURE 6·6
WORKSHOP EXERCISE

A STUDENT HAS WORKED OUT THE FOLLOWING PROBLEM:

```
 269 x
  23
----
 787
5380
----
6167
====
```

WORKING INDIVIDUALLY, GIVE THIS STUDENT A MARK OUT OF TEN

Those awarding zero argue that the answer is wrong and that wrong mathematical answers deserve zero. Those awarding other marks argue that substantial parts of the working are correct and deserve a proportion of the marks. However, all markers rapidly appreciate the importance of establishing marking guidelines to overcome this obvious problem of unreliable marking – even for an apparently straightforward piece of work!

Obviously more short-answer questions than essays can be fitted into a fixed time period. If one of the purposes of the assessment is to cover a wide content area, then short-answer questions have distinct advantages. Much the same may be said about multiple-choice questions but short-answer questions have the advantage of avoiding cueing and requiring students to supply an answer, rather than to select or to guess from a fixed number of options. The major limitation of the short-answer test is that it is not suitable for testing complex learning outcomes.

If you wish to employ short-answer questions you should take account of the points in Figure 6.7.

FIGURE 6.7
PROCEDURE FOR SETTING AND MARKING SHORT-ANSWER QUESTIONS

A Make the questions precise

Direct questions are better than incomplete statements.

If a numerical answer is required, indicate the units and degree of precision required.

B Prepare a structured marking sheet

Allocate marks or part-marks for the acceptable answer(s).

Be prepared to consider other equally acceptable answers, some of which you may not have predicted.

C Mark questions with the following points in mind:

Mark anonymously.

Complete the marking of one page of questions at a time.

Preferably have a different examiner for each page of questions.

3. OBJECTIVE TESTS

This generic term is used in education to include a variety of test formats in which the marking of the answers is objective. Some classifications include short-answer questions in this category. The term multiple-choice test is sometimes used synonymously with the term objective test. However, we

encourage you to use this more general term as it allows us to include a wide variety of test types, only one of which can be accurately described as 'multiple-choice'. Other commonly used examples of objective tests are the true–false and matching types.

The characteristics of such tests are the high reliability of the scoring, the rapidity of scoring and economy of staff time in this task, and the ability to test large content areas. They lend themselves to the development of banks of questions, thus further reducing the time of examination preparation in the long-term. These advantages have sometimes led to an over-reliance on objective tests and a failure to be critical in their use.

There is some debate about whether objective test items can be written to measure higher-level intellectual skills such as problem-solving. One view is that those very skilled in writing such items can do so (see Bloom, Hastings and Madaus). However, in one study there was little agreement among teachers and students with regard to the level of items in an examination. When students were asked to verbalize the process by which they arrived at their answer it was shown that they usually arrived at correct answers at a low taxonomic level (recall and recognition), irrespective of the teacher's taxonomic classification of the item. Problem-solving strategies were used by better students in answering items to which they did not immediately know the answer.

In many disciplines, especially in the sciences and technologies, it is almost certain that you will have to participate in some way in writing or administering objective tests. Therefore it is your responsibility to have quite a detailed knowledge about this type of assessment method. Though we will not be able to be comprehensive, we will attempt to provide you with enough information to do your job competently. This section will therefore contain more technical detail than the other sections in this chapter. We will have to leave it to you to judge how much of this detail is relevant to your needs.

Choosing the type of question

You must find out or decide which type of item you will be using. Objective items, as we have said before, can be classified into three groups: **true–false, multiple-choice** and **matching**. We would suggest you stick to the true–false and multiple-choice types and avoid the more complex matching types which, in some examinations, often seem to behave more like tests of IQ, rather than tests of the course content! For a variety of technical reasons, experts favour multiple-choice over other types of objective items.

True–false questions

Examples of true–false questions are shown in Figures 6.8 and 6.9.

FIGURE 6.8
EXAMPLE OF SIMPLE TRUE-FALSE ITEM

T F IN A NORMAL DISTRIBUTION THE MEDIAN, MODE AND MEAN COINCIDE

FIGURE 6.9
EXAMPLE OF MULTIPLE (CLUSTER) TRUE-FALSE ITEM.

IN A 40-YEAR-OLD PATIENT WITH MILD HYPERTENSION YOU WOULD CONSIDER COMMENCING TREATMENT WITH

T F ATENOLOL
T F HYDRALAZINE
T F BENDROFLUAZIDE
T F CLONIDINE
T F CAPTOPRIL

The **simple type** will obviously cause you the least problems in construction and scoring. The more complex **multiple type** (also known as the cluster type) is very popular because it allows a series of questions to be asked relating to a single stem or topic. Each question may be marked as a separate question. However, the questions may also be considered as a group with full marks given only if all the questions are correct and part-marks given if varying proportions of the questions are correct. Research has shown that the ranking of students is unaltered by the marking scheme used, so simplicity should be the guiding principle.

If you intend to use true–false questions you should take particular note of the points listed in Figure 6.10.

FIGURE 6.10
PROCEDURE FOR SETTING TRUE-FALSE QUESTIONS

Procedure

A Make sure that the content of the question is important and relevant and that the standard is appropriate to the group being tested.

B Use statements which are short, unambiguous and contain only one idea.

C Ensure that the statement is indeed unequivocally true or false.

D Avoid words which are give-aways to the correct answer, such as sometimes, always or never.

E Make sure that true statements and false statements are the same length and are written in approximately equal numbers.

F Avoid negative or double-negative statements.

Multiple-choice questions

An example of a simple multiple-choice question (MCQ) is shown in Figure 6.11.

FIGURE 6.11
EXAMPLE OF A SIMPLE MULTIPLE-CHOICE ITEM (ADAPTED FROM BLOOM AT AL)

'NEW CRITICISM' IS <u>MOST OFTEN</u> ASSOCIATED WITH WHICH OF THE FOLLOWING PAIRS OF TERMS?

1. AMBIGUITY AND PARADOX
2. COMEDY AND TRAGEDY
3. FEAR AND PITY
4. MYTH AND SYMBOL

The MCQ illustrated is made up of a stem (New criticism ... pairs of terms?) and four alternative answers. Of these alternatives one is correct and the others are known as 'distractors'.

One advantage of the MCQ over the true-false question is a reduction in the influence of guessing. Obviously, in a simple true-false question there is a 50 per cent chance of guessing the correct answer. In a one from four MCQ there is only a 25 per cent chance of doing so if all the distractors are working effectively. Unfortunately it is hard to achieve this ideal and exam-wise students may easily be able to eliminate one or two distractors and thus reduce the number of options from which

FIGURE 6.12
PROCEDURE FOR SETTING MULTIPLE-CHOICE QUESTIONS

Procedure

A Make sure that the content of the question is important and relevant and that the standard is appropriate to the group being tested.

B The main content of the question should be in the stem and the alternatives should be kept as short as possible.

C Eliminate redundant information from the stem.

D Ensure that each distractor is a plausible answer which cannot be eliminated from consideration because it is irrelevant or silly.

E Avoid giving clues to correct or incorrect responses which have nothing to do with the content of the question by:

- making sure correct and incorrect responses are of similar length;
- checking the grammar, particularly when the alternative is written as the completion of a statement in the stem;
- distributing the place of the correct response equally among positions 1 to 5 (or 1 to 4 as the case may be);
- avoiding 'always' or 'never'.

F Generally avoid 'all of the above' or 'none of the above' as alternatives.

G Avoid negatives.

H Do not try to write trick questions. For technical reasons use at least four alternative answers. Five are preferable but more are difficult to prepare.

they have to guess. Information about the effectiveness of the distractors is usually available after the examination if it has been computer-marked (see later section on item analysis). Some advocate the use of correction formulas for guessing but this does not – on balance – appear to be worth the effort.

If you intend to use multiple-choice questions you should take particular note of the points in Figure 6.12.

Context-dependent questions

Having mastered the basic principles of setting good objective items, you may wish to become more adventurous. It is possible to develop questions with a more complex stem which may require a degree of analysis before the answer is chosen. Such items are sometimes known as context-dependent multiple-choice questions. One or more multiple-choice questions are based on stimulus material which may be presented in the form of a diagram, a graph, a table of data, a statement from a text or research report, a photograph and so on. This approach is useful if one wishes to attempt to test the student's ability at a higher intellectual level than simple recognition and recall of factual information. An example of a context-dependent multiple-choice question is shown in Figure 6.13.

Putting together an objective test

This is the point where many tests come to grief. It is not enough simply to select 100 questions from the item bank or from among those recently prepared by your colleagues. The selection must be done with great care and must be based on the objectives of the course. A blueprint, or table of test specifications should be prepared which identifies the key topics of the course which must be tested. The number of questions to be allocated to each topic should then be determined according to its relative importance. Once this is done the job becomes easier. Sort out the objective items into the topics and select those which cover as many areas within the topic as possible. It is advisable to have a small working group at this stage to check the quality of the questions and to avoid your personal bias in the selection process. You may find that there are some topics for which there is an inadequate number or variety of questions. You should then commission

FIGURE 6·13
EXAMPLE OF
CONTEXT-DEPENDENT
QUESTION

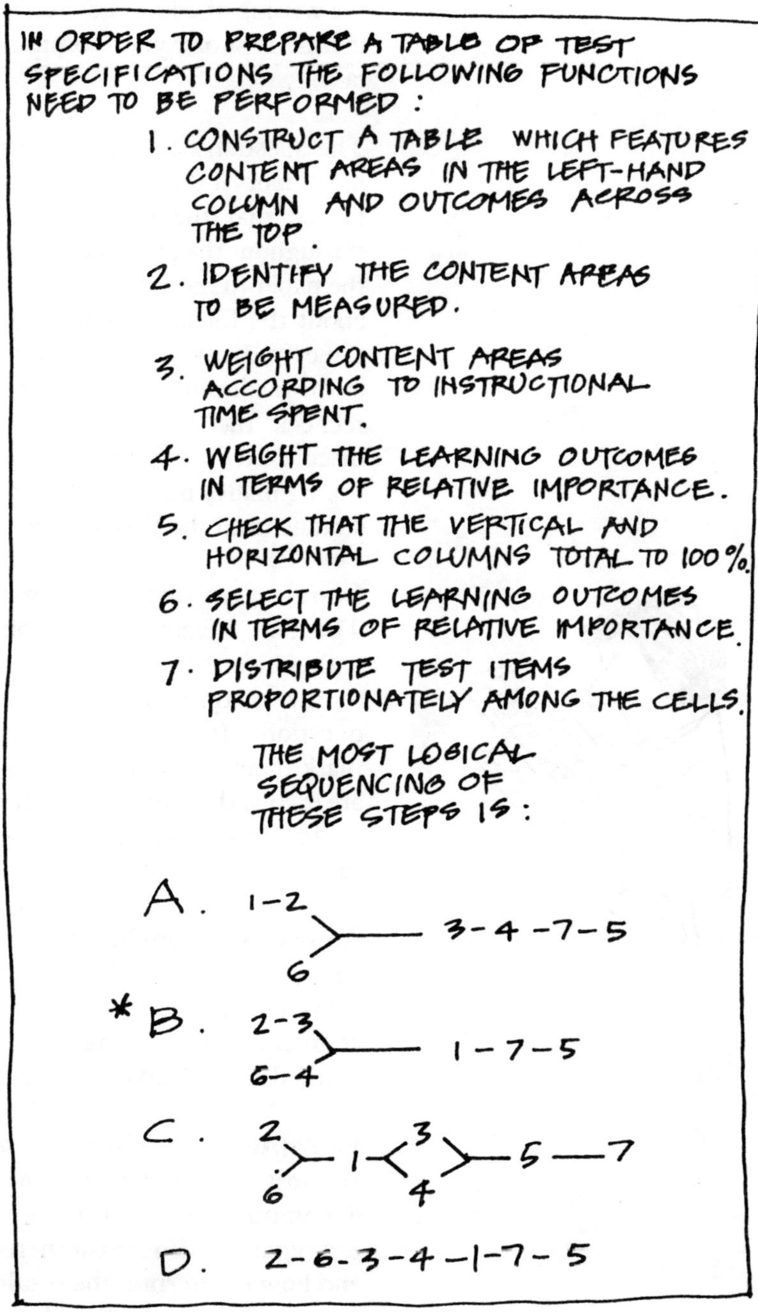

the writing of additional items from appropriate colleagues or, if time is short, your committee may have to undertake this task.

The questions should now be put in order. It is less confusing to students if the items for each topic are kept together. Check to see that the correct answers are randomly distributed throughout the paper and if not, re-order accordingly. Deliver the paper to the secretary for typing, with suitable instructions about the format required and the need for security. At the same time make sure that the 'Instructions to Students' section at the beginning of the paper is clear and accurate. Check and recheck the typed copy as errors are almost invariably discovered during the examination, a cause of much consternation. Finally, have the paper printed and arrange for secure storage until the time of the examination.

Scoring an objective test

The main advantage of the objective type tests is the rapidity with which scoring can be done. This requires some attention to the manner in which the students are to answer the questions. It is not usually appropriate to have the students mark their answers on the paper itself. When large numbers are involved a separate structured sheet should be used. Where facilities are available it is convenient to use answer sheets that can be directly scored by a computer or marking machine. However, a hand-marking answer sheet can easily be prepared. An overlay is produced by cutting out the positions of the correct responses. This can then be placed over the student's answer sheet and the correct responses are easily and rapidly counted. Before doing so ensure that the student has not marked more than one correct answer!

Computer-scoring and analysis

In most major undergraduate and postgraduate examinations a computer is used to score and analyse objective-type examinations. You must therefore be familiar with the process and how to interpret the results. Most institutional computers have programs which will produce lists of student results in alphabetical order and in order of merit. Raw scores can be manipulated to produce for you a wide range of statistical data.

The computer can, for example, provide information on the number of questions answered by each student, the mean and standard deviation for the class and a reliability statistic such as a Kuder–Richardson test for internal consistency. If necessary, the data can be re-worked to provide statistics on subsets of questions such as those covering separate topics.

The item analysis: This is a component of the computer printout which warrants detailed discussion because of the problems it seems to cause many teachers. It contains valuable information for the person who has been responsible for constructing test times and assembling the examination. The item analysis provides numerical and statistical information on each item in the test.

A typical output of an item analysis for a multiple-choice question is shown in Figure 6.14.

FIGURE 6·14
EXAMPLE OF AN ITEM ANALYSIS

Percentage correct of all students	Discrimination *R* biserial	Discrimination index	Difficulty index	Item no.
54.55	0.39	0.60	45.45	1
	Significant at 5.0% level			

Number of students answering each alternative (* correct answer)

Group	Omitted	A	B	C*	D
Upper	1	0	0	39	2
Middle	4	0	0	31	35
Lowcr	6	3	5	14	14
TOTAL	11	3	5	84	51

The **discrimination index** compares the performance of the students in the whole test with their performance on each item within the test. The students are divided, on the basis of their overall performance in the test, into upper, middle and lower groups. In most item analyses, for statistical reasons, the proportions happen to be 27, 46 and 27 per cent respectively.

Looking at the example you will see that in the upper group 39 students answered correctly while in the lower group only 14 students answered correctly. The discrimination index is simply calculated from the following formula:

$$D = \frac{R_U - R_L}{\frac{1}{2}\,T}$$

Where R_U = number of students in upper group answering correctly

R_L = number of students in lower group answering correctly

T = total number of students answering correctly

From the example in Figure 6.14:

$$D = \frac{39 - 14}{\frac{1}{2} \times 84} = \frac{25}{42} = 0.60$$

The discrimination index may have a value between +1 and -1. An item which did not discriminate between the two groups would produce an index of zero. An item where the lower group of students performed better than the top group of students would produce a negative index. Should the latter occur there is usually something seriously wrong with the item or there has been a technical or clerical error (eg the correct answer has been incorrectly indicated on the mark sheet or computer form). Generally speaking, one is looking for items to have a discrimination index of above 0.40, and certainly not less than 0.20, but an item should not necessarily be discarded because it fails to reach this level. It is always important to look at the content of the question when reviewing an item analysis.

The **discrimination *R* biserial** (also known as the point-biserial correlation coefficient) correlates the scores obtained on a particular item with the scores obtained on the test as a whole. A test of significance can be applied which is equivalent to a *t*-test of the difference between two means. High values indicate that the students who performed well on the whole test also performed well on that item and that students who performed badly on the whole test also performed badly on that question. These values are meaningful only if they are significant at the 5 per cent level. Interpretation of this statistic remains a matter for your judgement, just as with the discrimination index.

The **difficulty index** is also calculated for you. It is simply the percentage of students who answered the item incorrectly. Some care is needed here, as in some item analyses this term is used to express the percentage of students who answered **correctly**. In our example, such confusion should not arise as both are provided. An item difficulty index of around 30 per cent or a percentage correct of around 70 per cent is suggested for a one from five choice item; and 25 and 75 per cent, respectively, for a one from four choice item.

The **efficiency of distractors** can be judged by inspecting the table. Only one of the distractors (D) attracted responses from the upper group, but all distractors (A, B and D) attracted responses from the lower group. However, distractor A only attracted three responses and has essentially converted a one from four MCQ into a one from three MCQ. The question should thus be reviewed and distractor A replaced with a more plausible alternative. Many questions will be found that are much worse than this where two or even three distractors serve no useful purpose thus increasing the likelihood of correctly guessing the right answer.

4. DIRECT OBSERVATION

Direct observation of the student performing a technical or an interpersonal skill in the real, simulated or examination setting would appear to be the most valid way of assessing such skills. Unfortunately, the reliability of these observations is likely to be seriously low. This is particularly so in the complex interpersonal area where no alternative form of assessment is available. Nevertheless, in professional courses it is essential to continue to make assessments of the student's performance, if only to indicate to the student your commitment to these vital skills. In doing so, you would be well advised to use the information predominantly for feedback rather than for important decision-making.

Various ways have been suggested by which these limitations might be minimized. One is to improve the method of scoring and another is to improve the performance of the observer. The former involves the design of checklists and rating forms.

Checklists

A checklist is basically a two-point rating scale. Evidence suggests that the reliability of a checklist decreases when there are more than four points on the scale. The assessor has to decide whether each component on the list is present/absent; adequate/inadequate; satisfactory/unsatisfactory. Only if each component is very clearly defined and readily observable can a checklist be reliable. They are particularly useful for assessing technical skills. An example of a checklist is given in Figure 6.4.

Rating forms

Rating forms come in many styles. The essential feature is that the observer is required to make a judgement along a scale which may be continuous or intermittent. They are widely used to assess behaviour or performance because no other methods are usually available, but the subjectivity of the assessment is an unavoidable problem. Because of this, multiple independent ratings of the same student undertaking the same activity are essential if any sort of justice is to be done. The examples in Figure 6.15 show several alternative structures for rating the same ability. They are derived from published formats used to obtain information about ward performance of specialist trainees or interns in the medical area. The component skill being assessed is 'Obtaining the data base' and only one subcomponent (obtaining information from the patient) is illustrated.

Format 3 is the one we would recommend for two reasons. The first is that there is an attempt to provide descriptive anchor points which may be helpful in clarifying for the observer what standards should be applied. The second is a more pragmatic one. In a study we undertook, it was the format most frequently preferred by experienced clinical raters.

FIGURE 6·15
EXAMPLES OF RATING FORMS

Format 1

	Top quarter	Upper-middle quarter	Lower-middle quarter	Bottom quarter
Obtaining information from the patient	4	3	2	1

Format 2

Obtaining information from the patient

☐	☐	☐	☐	☐	☐
Very effective	Effective	Reasonable	Poor	Inadequate	Unable to judge

Format 3

Obtaining information from the patient

☐	☐	☐	☐
Little or no information obtained	Some information obtained; major errors or omissions	Adequate performance; most information elicited	Very thorough exploration of patient's problems

Improving the performance of the observer

It has often been claimed that training of raters will improve reliability. This seems to make sense but what evidence there is shows that training makes remarkably little difference! A recent study of our own suggested that a better approach might be to select raters who are inherently more consistent than others. Common sense dictates that observers should be adequately briefed on the rating form and that they should not be asked to rate on aspects of the student's performance that they have not observed.

5. ORAL

The oral or viva-voce examination has for centuries been the predominant method, and sometimes the only method, used to assess medical students. The traditional oral, which gives considerable freedom to the examiner to vary the questions asked from student to student and to exercise personal bias, has consistently been shown to be very unreliable. One major study of oral examinations showed that the correlation between different examiners was overall no greater than would have occurred by chance. There is no reason to believe that oral examinations conducted in other disciplines would stand up any better to similar scrutiny.

Without doubt, face-to-face interaction between student and examiner provides a unique opportunity to test language and interactive skills which cannot be assessed in any other way. However, these skills are not usually the focus of attention and several studies have shown that the majority of questions in oral examinations require little more than the recall of isolated fragments of information, something more easily and more reliably assessed by objective written tests.

We would recommend that reliance on oral examination be considerably reduced unless, of course, it is obviously the only valid assessment method; for example, in the speaking of a foreign language. It might be possible to incorporate many of the activities currently assessed in oral examinations into the objective-structured approach discussed in the next section. However, orals may be appropriate where one wishes to discriminate among top students by providing a challenge with in-depth questioning.

Should you wish to retain oral examinations then certain steps should be undertaken to minimize the likely problems, as outlined in Figure 6.16.

Surprising as it may seem, examiners used to traditional oral exams seem to appreciate this structured approach as most are well aware of their own limitations. When the content is

FIGURE 6.16
PROCEDURE FOR CONDUCTING ORAL EXAMINATIONS

Procedure

A Standardize the content

- Define the content to be tested.
- If it is a theoretical oral get the examiners together beforehand and prepare a standard set of questions to be asked of each student. These should be identical if examined students can be kept apart from students yet to be examined. If not, the questions should be equivalent in content and difficulty.
- If it is a practical test the same principles should apply but in this case the students should be faced with similar or equivalent situations and asked to perform the same tasks.

B Reduce the examiner inconsistency

- Prepare structured marking sheets or rating forms and brief examiners in their use.
- Use as many examiners as possible. In other words, break down the oral examination into several shorter sessions rather than one long session.
- Ensure that each student gets asked the agreed questions and is given approximately the same time to answer them.
- Ensure that each examiner marks independently and avoids discussing individual students until all marks are collated.
- Establish controls for potential bias due to differences in student's and examiner's age, sex and ethnicity.

standardized they become much more confident of assessing the differences between students. Therefore, do not be frightened to suggest such changes, even in the most conservative teaching department.

6. STRUCTURED PRACTICAL ASSESSMENT

In recent years there has been a search for new approaches to assessment. One of the most interesting of these developments has been the 'objective structured clinical (practical) examination' initially described by Harden and his colleagues in Dundee and subsequently developed by ourselves and others as an integral part of medical examinations.

The structured examination is essentially an administrative structure into which a variety of test methods can be incorporated. The aim is to test a wide range of skills in an objective fashion.

The students proceed through a series of 'stations' and undertake a variety of practical and clinical tasks. Marking sheets and checklists are prepared beforehand to improve the reliability of scoring. All students are thus examined on the same content and marked on the same criteria by the same examiners. As in any form of assessment, the definition of the content to be tested and the preparation of good test items is essential if a high degree of validity and reliability are to be obtained.

Though such examinations are particularly well suited to medical education, the method is now being applied in other disciplines where practical skills have to be reliably assessed.

Should you wish to consider introducing such an approach you should read the articles given in the references and adapt the ideas to your own discipline.

7. SELF-ASSESSMENT

By 'self-assessment' we mean an assessment system which involves the students in establishing the criteria and standards they will apply to their work and then in making judgements about the degree to which they have been met.

We believe that the skill of being able to make realistic evaluations of the quality of one's work is one that every graduate should have. Yet, in conventional courses, few opportunities are provided for self-assessment skills to be learnt and developed.

The introduction of self-assessment practices into existing courses has been shown to be feasible and desirable. Whether marks generated in this way should count towards a final grade is an undecided issue. Nevertheless, there is little doubt that self-assessment, used primarily to improve the students' understanding of their own ability and performance, is worthwhile educationally and encourages openness and honesty about assessment.

If you wish to embark on a trial scheme you must first set about the task of establishing criteria and standards. This can be done at a series of small group meetings attended by staff and students. Both must agree on the criteria to be applied to the students' work. To help focus on this task you might have students reflect on questions such as:

How would you distinguish good from inadequate work? What would characterize a good assignment in this course?

Once criteria have been specified, students use them to judge their own performance. Marks are awarded with reference to each criterion and a statement justifying the mark should be included. An alternative is to contrast their own mark with one given to them by a peer. The teacher may also mark a random sample to establish controls and to discourage cheating or self-delusion. We urge you to give this new method of assessment serious consideration and suggest you obtain a copy of the booklet by Boud.

REPORTING THE RESULTS OF ASSESSMENT

In many major examinations you will be required to report the results as a final mark or grade based on a number of different assessment methods. What usually happens is that marks from these different assessments are simply added or averaged and the final mark or grade awarded. Simple though this approach may be, it can introduce serious distortions. Factors contributing to this problem may be differing distributions of marks in each subtest; varying numbers of questions; differing levels of difficulty; and a failure to appropriately weight each component.

The answer is to convert each raw subscore to a standardized score. This is not the place to do more than alert you to the need to do so and refer you to a text on educational measurement (eg Mehrens and Lehmann; Gronlund; or Clift and Imrie) or to advise you to enlist the aid of an educational statistician, who can usually be found by contacting the teaching unit in your institution.

GUIDED READING

There are many useful general texts on educational measurement. Two which provide straightforward accounts of the principles and procedures of assessment are: W A Mehrens and I J Lehmann's *Measurement and Evaluation in Education and Psychology* (3rd Edn), Holt, Rinehart & Winston, New York, 1984; and N E Gronlund's *Measurement and Evaluation in Teaching* (5th Edn), Macmillan, New York, 1985. Both have useful discussions of broad assessment considerations such as objectives, planning, reliability, validity and scoring, and also provide a wide range of examples of test items that you could use as models for your own tests.

Another book which you may find useful is the *Handbook on Formative and Summative Evaluation of Student Learning* by B S Bloom, J T Hastings and G F Madaus, McGraw-Hill, New York, 1971. This two-part volume is particularly useful for the development of test items and contains numerous examples designed to test achievement at different levels of Bloom's taxonomy of educational objectives. *Assessing Students, Appraising Teaching* by J C Clift and B W Imrie, Croom Helm, London, 1981, is another general overview text that we recommend because of the many examples of test items relevant to higher education and a very helpful section on marking and awarding grades.

Books and articles referred to in this chapter:

'Assessment of practical skills: the objective structured practical examination (OSPE)' by R M Harden and R G Cairncross, *Studies in Higher Education*, **5:** 187–96, 1980.

'Eight years' experience with a structured clinical examination' by D I Newble, *Medical Education*, **22:** 200–4, 1988.

Implementing Student Self-Assessment (Green Guide No 4) by David Boud, Higher Education Research and Development Society of Australasia, C/- Tertiary Education Research Centre, University of New South Wales, Kensington, NSW 2033, Australia, 1986. The theory and practice of self- and peer-assessment are admirably treated in this booklet. We strongly recommend a reading of this work because of its potential importance as an educational tool within the context of assessment.

For the assessment of practical and laboratory skills, there is an excellent chapter in D Boud, J Dunn and E Hegarty-Hazel, *Teaching in Laboratories*, SRHE/NFER-Nelson, Open University, Milton Keynes, UK, 1986. This chapter also addresses fundamental issues of test planning as well as providing some very helpful examples of test items.

Chapter 7 Preparing Teaching Materials and Using Teaching Aids

INTRODUCTION

In your teaching career you will use quite a wide range of audiovisual and printed teaching materials. How these materials can be economically and effectively produced and how you might use them is the focus of this chapter.

The fundamental criterion for judging the effectiveness of your teaching material is its audibility and/or visibility. If that seems too obvious to warrant mention, have a look at some of the materials used by others: sound recordings that are so distorted that they cannot be understood; slides with excessive amounts of tiny detail that cannot be read on the screen; blackboards that look like someone's doodle pad; and faded handouts that cannot be read. Exaggeration? It does happen! When it does, it seriously interferes with the effectiveness of teaching. Attention to the way in which the material is produced and how it is used in teaching will eliminate many of these problems.

BASIC PRINCIPLES OF TEACHING MATERIAL PREPARATION

Whether you are preparing a simple handout or a videocassette, there are some basic principles that can be incorporated into your design and preparation that will enhance the quality and effectiveness of the material.

Relevance

Materials should be relevant to the purpose for which they were created and to the students' level of understanding of the topic. Complex handouts distributed at the end of a lecture and never referred to by the teacher are classic offenders of this principle.

Linkage

An introduction is usually required to establish the purpose of the material and to link it with what it is reasonable to expect students to know already.

Simplicity

Simplicity in the use of language and design, the avoidance of needless qualifications and the use of suitable abstractions of complex situations can be positive aids to understanding. For example, a simple line diagram may be more helpful in an explanation than a full-colour photograph or a multihued computer-generated slide.

Emphasis

Emphatic 'signs' can be incorporated into all teaching materials to stress important ideas, to indicate a change in the development of an argument, or to identify new material. Examples of emphasis include: headings and underlinings in print; the use of colour on charts and slides; the use of pointers and close-ups in video; and statements such as 'this is a major factor' on a sound recording.

Consistency in the use of pattern and style

Students acquire a 'feel' for the particular style you use to present material. Needless changing of style is only going to confuse them. This is one of the reasons why imported materials, such as video-recordings, may achieve less impact than similar materials produced by a local teacher.

TYPES OF TEACHING MATERIALS AND AIDS

With these basic principles in mind, the preparation and use of several basic types of teaching materials and aids will now be described. These are:

1 The overhead projector

2 The blackboard and whiteboard

3 The 35 mm slide projector
4 Video and film
5 Tape–slide presentations
6 Printed materials

This list is by no means exhaustive. In keeping with the general thrust of this book, the intention is to get you started and to help you develop some confidence in the basic aspects of your teaching work.

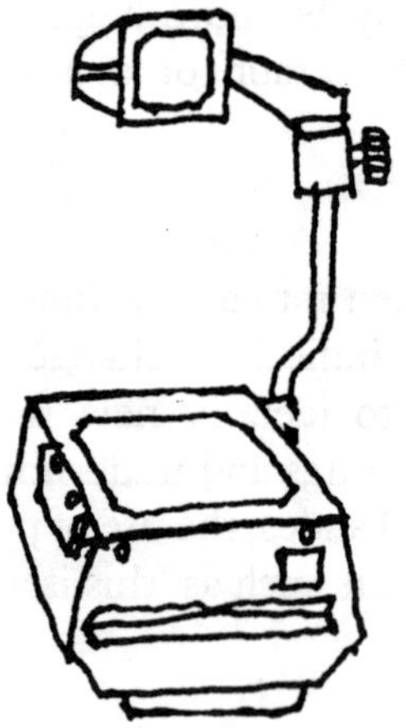

1. THE OVERHEAD PROJECTOR

This valuable visual aid can project a wide range of transparency materials and silhouettes of opaque objects on to a screen positioned behind the teacher. Because it can project both written and diagrammatic information, it reduces your need to engage in detailed descriptions and increases the opportunities for discussion with students. It also allows you to indicate things on the transparency without turning your back to the audience, an advantage over using a slide projector.

The full benefit of the overhead projector will not be realized in your teaching unless you give careful attention to three things: the preparation of the transparency, the way the projector is set up in a room or lecture theatre, and the way you actually use it. We shall now turn to a consideration of each of these matters.

Transparency preparation

Figure 7.1 shows what a transparency looks like. It consists of an acetate sheet mounted on to a cardboard frame. Additional sheets of acetate on the same frame are known as overlays.

Overlays are particularly helpful to build up an idea as a presentation develops. The following methods of making transparencies are available.

Felt pens: Felt pens containing water-soluble or permanent ink are available for making transparencies. Information is printed or drawn directly on to an acetate sheet. A suggested

FIGURE 7:1
EXAMPLE OF
TRANSPARENCY

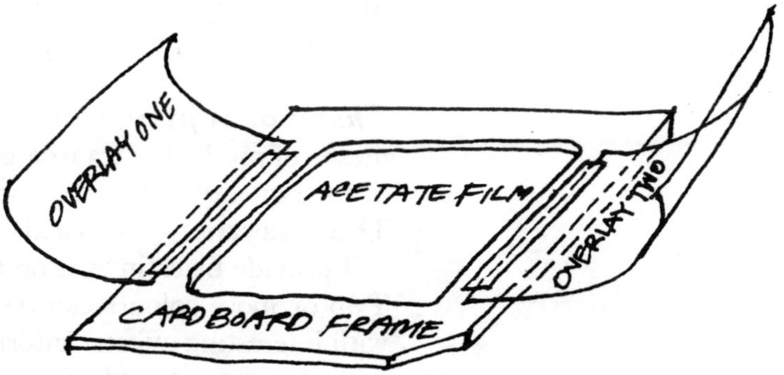

5MM LETTERS

procedure is to mount the acetate sheet on to a frame with adhesive tape, place a piece of ruled paper underneath the acetate as a guide and write on to the sheet. Another sheet of clean paper placed under your hand will prevent smudges from appearing on the acetate. Lettering should be no smaller than 5 mm in height and preferably larger. Use black, blue, brown or green pens for lettering, avoiding red, orange and yellow which are difficult to read at a distance.

Graphics and word-processing packages: Microcomputer software packages give you a means of producing master sheets for transparencies. Graphics packages allow you to prepare diagrams as well. Some excellent software of this type is available in the public domain. Provided the printout is of sufficient quality (a laser printer is best) and large fonts are chosen in setting up the page, excellent transparencies can be produced.

For the really avant-garde, it is now possible to obtain an attachment for an overhead projector which allows an image to be generated by a microcomputer and projected directly on to the screen.

Adhesive films and letters: You can use rub-down materials such as Letraset directly on to an acetate sheet if you wish to give a professional-looking finish. This is time-consuming if you have to do it yourself and should be restricted to the preparation of transparencies to be used repeatedly or in prestigious meetings. A much easier method is to use a lettering machine. With this device, bold letters are punched on to a clear tape and then transferred to the transparency.

Materials prepared in these ways are best used in conjunction with one of the following processes.

Thermal copying: Thermal copiers offer an economical means of producing transparencies, providing your original is of good quality, with bold black lettering and thick black lines. There is a variety of thermal films from which to select. These will provide black images on a clear or coloured background. Two or more colours can be combined in one transparency with interesting effects. Information on specific films and the procedure you should follow is supplied by manufacturers or can be obtained from a visual aid consultant.

Photocopying: Many plain-paper copiers will now accept acetate sheets, enabling the production of black and white transparencies at the touch of a button. It is essential that the type of sheet selected is suitable for use with the copier available and that the original material is large and clear. Lettering, for example, must be at least 5 mm in height. Avoid the temptation to make overheads directly from books or from ordinary typed materials. If you wish to use such material you should first make an enlargement. This is possible on many photocopying machines. An alternative is to photograph the original, get it enlarged and use this to produce the transparency.

Other uses of the overhead projector

There are other, less orthodox ways in which you can use the overhead projector. Silhouettes of cardboard cut-outs or solid objects can be projected on to the screen. These may be co-ordinated with a prepared transparency. Transparent or translucent materials such as liquids in test-tubes or biological specimens mounted on, or contained in, clear containers can also be prepared.

The points listed in Figure 7.2 should be kept in mind when preparing an overhead transparency.

Setting up and using the overhead projector

In some situations you will have flexibility in setting up the projector and screen. It is usual to place the projector so that it

FIGURE 7.2
GUIDELINES FOR MAKING AN EFFECTIVE OVERHEAD TRANSPARENCY

Guidelines

★ Limit each transparency to one main idea. Several simple transparencies are preferable to a complicated one.

★ Reduce tabulated data to essential or to rounded figures. A single graph or diagram may be preferable.

★ Typed originals must be photographed and enlarged. To help in this, use a typing template - a bold rectangular outline with an aspect ratio of 4:3. An outline measuring 120 mm wide and 90 mm high is suitable for this.

★ As an alternative to typing, consider using a word-processor and photocopier.

is adjacent to the lectern or table from which you are working. Ensure that the projected image is square on the screen and free from angular and colour distortions. Angular distortions in the vertical axis can be overcome by tilting the top of the screen forward. Colour distortions, such as red or blue in the corners of the projected image, can usually be remedied by making an adjustment to the lamp. A control for this is often inside the projector. It is important to turn the electricity off at the power point before the adjustment is attempted.

Whenever a projector is moved, or before a presentation is commenced, the focus and position of the image must be checked. Once this is done, it is usually unnecessary to look at the screen again, particularly if you use a pen or pointer directly on the transparency. This enables you to maintain eye-contact with students. If you wish to mask out part of the transparency, place a sheet of paper between the film and the glass stage of the projector; the weight of the transparency should prevent the paper from moving or falling away.

Remember to allow students plenty of time to read what you have projected. Many teachers find this difficult to do. One way is to read carefully the transparency to yourself word for word. As well, make sure that anything you have to say complements the transparency. Do not expect students to listen to you and to look at something on the screen that is only vaguely related to what is being said. It is advisable to have the lamp on only when a transparency is being used in your teaching, otherwise the projected image or the large area of white light will distract the students' attention.

Storage of transparencies

Your transparencies will last many years if carefully used and stored, so the effort in making them professionally is well worthwhile. A dust- and scratch-free environment is best for storage. You can use the cardboard boxes that the mounts are sold in for this or make a protective wallet from two manilla folders sealed together with tape. Some teachers store a whole lecture in this way and interleave their transparencies with their lecture notes.

2. THE BLACKBOARD

The blackboard (which these days may be green) is still a commonly used visual aid and the one that you are likely to use quite frequently, unless you rely exclusively on the overhead projector. Few teachers give much thought to the material they put on the board or to the way they use it. This is a pity. The results of the work are often ugly and indecipherable. Well-planned and well-used blackboard work is a delight to see and is a valuable ally in conveying information accurately and clearly to your students.

Preparation

It is important to think ahead about your use of the board and make suitable notations in your teaching notes. Plan your use of the board by dividing the available space into a number of sections. Each section is then used for a specific purpose such as references, diagrams, a summary of the structure of the lecture and so on.

Using a blackboard

Some guidelines for using a blackboard are given in Figure 7.3.

The whiteboard

The principles of blackboard use and preparation apply also to whiteboards. Do take care to use the correct pens with a whiteboard as some can ruin its surface. Also take care when cleaning a whiteboard. A dry cloth is often adequate but

FIGURE 7.3
GUIDELINES FOR USING A BLACKBOARD (AFTER HALL AND CANNON)

Guidelines

- Start a presentation with a clean board. Downward strokes with a duster will prevent wide spreading of chalk dust.
- Try to avoid talking and writing on the blackboard at the same time. When speaking, look at the students, not at the board.
- Face the board squarely and move across the board when writing. This will assist in writing horizontally.
- Stand aside when writing or drawing is completed to enable students to see the blackboard.
- Concise information in skeleton note form is preferred to a 'newspaper' effect.
- Underline headings and important or unfamiliar words to give visual emphasis.
- Always give students a chance to copy down the information you have taken time to put on the blackboard (if it is intended that they should have a copy).
- Use colours liberally but with discretion. Yellow and white are suitable colours for most written work. Use red, dark blue and green chalk sparingly as they are difficult to see and difficult to erase.

sometimes you may need to use water, detergent or perhaps methylated spirits. Never use an abrasive cleaner as it will scratch the surface and do irreparable damage.

The colour of the pens you use is important. Black, dark blue and green are best. Avoid yellow, red and light colours as these can be difficult to read from a distance.

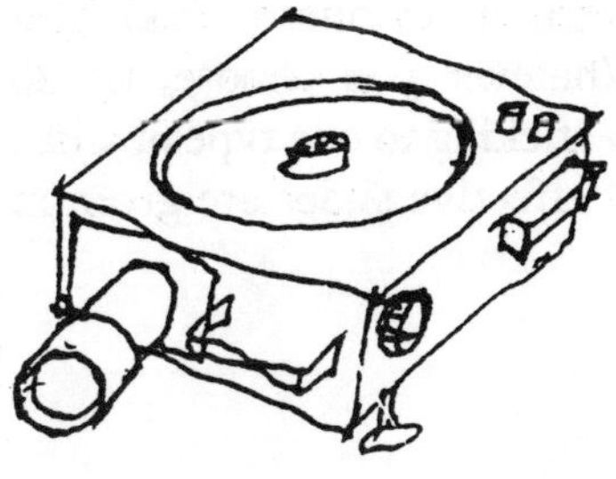

3. THE 35 MM SLIDE PROJECTOR

Much of what has been said about the overhead projector applies to slide projection. However, you will recognize that there are important differences between the two and that one of these is that full-colour images can be used in slides. This may be an advantage but with some material it may also be a disadvantage, unless the students' level of understanding is sufficient to enable them to see what is relevant and pertinent in the material you are using. Slide interpretation can be aided by including in the photograph an appropriate reference point or a scale.

Slide preparation

The major error in slide making is to assume that legibility in one medium, such as a table in a book or a journal, ensures slide legibility. Slides made from printed materials frequently contain too much detail and fine line work to enable them to be projected satisfactorily. This means that you may have to have artwork redrawn and new lettering added. Check any slides in your possession for legibility. A useful rule of thumb is that a slide which can be read without a magnifier is generally satisfactory. A better method is to go with a colleague to a large lecture theatre, project your slides and check to see if all details are legible and understandable at the rear of the auditorium.

When making slides, avoid the temptation to put all the details into the slide. If it is important for students to have all the details, provide these in a handout so that they can refer to it and keep it for reference. This ensures that they have accurate information on hand.

University or college photographers will advise you on the different processes available to produce your slides. These processes will usually include simple black-on-white slides, colour slides and diazo slides (white against blue, green or red backgrounds, the blue being preferred for clarity). Your institution may also be able to help you produce computer-generated colour slides of high quality. Another attractive way to prepare slides is to obtain negatives (white-on-black) and colour the white sections in by hand using coloured marking pens or translucent coloured paper designed for this purpose. The possibility exists for using separate colours to highlight different points on the slide. Whatever you choose, try to achieve a degree of consistency by sticking to one type of slide. Guidelines for the preparation of effective slides are given in Figure 7.4.

FIGURE 7.4 GUIDELINES FOR MAKING EFFECTIVE SLIDES

Guidelines

- Limit each slide to one main idea.
- Reduce tabulated data to essential or to rounded figures. Simple graphs and diagrams are to be preferred.
- When making new slides use a template with an aspect ratio of 3:2. An outline for typing of about 140 mm x 95 mm or 230 mm x 150 mm for artwork is suitable.

Setting up and using the slide projector

Slide projection equipment is normally part of the standard fixtures in a lecture theatre these days so the question of setting up does not usually arise. If it does, locate the projector and screen with care to give the best view to students and so that it is convenient for you to operate the projector and room lights with a minimum of fuss. A remote control device will be an invaluable aid.

Slide projection

Before loading your slides into a cartridge or carousel, carefully plan the sequence of their use. If your teaching is to be interspersed with slides, consider using black slides to separate your material and to avoid having to keep turning the projector on and off or leaving an inappropriate slide on view. Black slides are simply pieces of opaque film mounted in a slide frame to block off light to the screen and can be easily made from exposed film. If you plan to use the same slide on more than one occasion during a presentation, arrange to have duplicates made to save you and your students the agony of having to search back and forth through a slide series.

It is essential to have your slides marked or 'spotted' for projection (see Figure 7.5). As a check, the slides should be upside down and emulsion side (ie the dull side) towards the screen. When showing your slides, it is rarely necessary to turn off all the lights. Remember that students may wish to take notes and so you should plan to leave some lights on or to dim the main lights. Further advice on using slides is given in Chapter 2 on presenting a paper at a conference.

FIGURE 7.5
PROCEDURE FOR "SPOTTING" SLIDES

Procedure

1. Place your slides on a light box (an overhead projector is ideal for this) so that the image is the same way up as it is to appear on the screen.
2. Turn the slide upside down.
3. Mark or number the slide in the top right-hand corner.

4. VIDEO AND FILM

Of all the teaching materials at your disposal you will probably find that video and, to a less extent, film, will give you the most flexibility and the opportunity to experiment with novel approaches to teaching. This is particularly true of the material you make yourself but you should become familiar with the range of suitable commercially available materials before embarking on a career as a producer. You will find that several subject areas are well catered for in this regard.

Although the uses of video and film are similar, video does offer you several additional advantages such as ease of production and relative cheapness. These have tended to make this medium rather more popular and flexible than film. Incidentally, it is important to explain what we mean by 'video' and to distinguish video from 'television'. **Television** generally refers to the process of transmitting and receiving pictures and sound via broadcast. Television programmes are made in large studios with elaborate production systems or they may be broadcast films. Television has had some educational uses but, because of rigid time-scheduling of broadcasts and the cost, has found little acceptance in education. This has changed to some extent with the arrival of the videocassette-recorder which has enabled broadcasts to be recorded for later use but this, of course, is usually in breach of copyright laws. **Video** is a term applied to locally made material produced in a university or college studio or by the teacher using a single camera and recorder system. It is usually of a lesser technical standard than broadcast television. Video is generally produced with a restricted audience in mind.

Using video and film in teaching

As with many teaching aids the uses are restricted only by your imagination and by the resources at your disposal. Some of the potential uses of video and film are described below.

As introductory material: Video and film can be used at the start of a course or series of lectures to stimulate interest, to provide an overview and to form a basis for further teaching. For example, a film on the effects of cigarette smoking could be used as a point of departure for a discourse on lung cancer in health education courses.

As a major source of information: A constant flow of new ideas, techniques and procedures are a fact of life in many disciplines. Video and film can be used to disseminate this new information to your students or to professional meetings with which you may be involved. A further advantage of these media is that they can provide the viewer with vicarious experience where this might be difficult or dangerous to obtain at first hand.

As a means of modelling: This use is similar to the previous one, but you may find it helpful to produce material which demonstrates a technique or procedure in a clear step-by-step manner that students can watch and emulate at their own pace. An example might be a demonstration of how to conduct an appraisal interview in a management course.

As a stimulus for discussion: Short open-ended sections of video or film can be made to stimulate discussion among students (trigger films). Students respond to the material as it is presented and the stimulus and the response are then discussed. This we have found to be valuable for starting discussion about attitudes dealing with emotional situations. Sometimes it is possible to locate suitable stimulus material in old films that would otherwise have no use. Trigger films are commercially available.

As a means of distribution and relay: Carefully placed video-cameras can be used to distribute pictures to a separate viewing room or even to relay them to remote locations. An obvious example of this is their use in operating theatres to enable a large number of medical students to witness an operation. Such an approach certainly provides advantages over the lecture theatre galleries of yester-year.

As an information storage system: Video has an important role to play in storing information for later teaching or for research use. For example, a recording can be made (with permission) of a particularly important historical event for subsequent review and analysis.

As a means of assembling visual and audio information: Video can be extremely helpful if you want to assemble a variety of information in one 'package'. Film clips, stills, models, interviews, recorded sounds and graphics can be recorded, assembled and edited to make a teaching programme. You will need to obtain the advice of your audiovisual department before embarking on such a project.

As a magnification medium: Many teachers find that video is a handy tool to 'blow-up' the action or to display pictures of a demonstration. These can, of course, be recorded if needed for subsequent use.

These examples of video and film use are by no means exhaustive nor are they mutually exclusive in their application. For example, in teaching dentistry, video is used to magnify materials, to distribute and display this in a large laboratory (thus ensuring that all students are seeing the same thing) and sometimes to record the information as a source for student self-study.

The advent of the home video and the videodisc is an indication that the video, like the computer, is destined to play a large role in education. Our experience with producing videodiscs is that this medium provides two significant advantages for the teacher. First, because of its enormous visual storage capacity, the disc can be used to 'bank' large numbers of slides, film or video sequences in a readily accessible and durable way. Second, when used with a computer, the student can work interactively with the visual material. The exploration of this exciting development is just beginning. Videodiscs for this purpose are expensive to produce but copies are relatively cheap. They are now becoming available commercially.

Making educational videos

In this section it is assumed that you have been asked or have decided to make a video to illustrate some aspect of your teaching. Depending on the complexity of the proposal, you may use a simple camera and recorder system available in your department or decide to use the services of an audiovisual unit. In the latter case you will be able to draw on their guidance in going about the production. Nevertheless, there are a number of considerations in making a video which are outlined here to prepare you for discussions with producers from the unit or, alternatively, to help you undertake the work on your own.

Planning: As with most teaching, careful planning will repay dividends in production time and in the quality of the product. The first step in planning is to commit your thoughts to paper by writing down the story-line. This is simply a statement of the main message you wish to communicate in your programme. The story-line can be as brief as a sentence or two but should be no more than half a page or so in length. You may wish to sketch in some ideas to help you visualize the content. Once you are satisfied with your story-line, turn your attention to reviewing the educational, technical and administrative considerations in producing and using the video in your teaching. We have found it helpful to pose a series of questions to focus on these considerations.

The **educational** questions are these:

- What are students expected to learn by viewing the proposed video?
- How is the topic taught at present?
- Why is video being substituted for the present method of teaching?
- Is video an appropriate medium to achieve the aims?
- How will the proposed video be used in teaching (eg will students be expected to carry out any discussion or exercises after viewing it)?

- ★ Will the material be suitable for the students' level of understanding and skill?
- ★ How will the effectiveness of the video be assessed?

The **technical** questions are:

- ⇨ Is the technical quality of the production and playback equipment adequate to show the detail and colour you require?
- ⇨ In what format is the finished video required? (U-Matic, VHS, Beta, or videodisc will be among the main alternatives here.)
- ⇨ Are the technical resources available to you adequate for the task?
- ⇨ Are additional materials such as graphics, slides and sound-effects required?

Finally, the important **administrative** questions to consider are:

- Are there sufficient resources of people, equipment and money available to undertake the work?
- When is the finished work required?
- Who (if not yourself) is to accept responsibility for the production?
- Is the production timetable clear to all parties involved and realistic in terms of other commitments?

These, then, are some of the questions you need to consider before embarking on your work. If you intend to work alone, it will be helpful to discuss at least the educational questions with a colleague and you may need to seek some advice on a number of technical matters.

Scripting: The script is the detailed plan of your programme. It indicates the relationship between visuals and commentary. The script is used to guide those making the

programme in such things as visual sequences, narration, materials required and so on.

In preparing a script, you will find the use of blank white cards invaluable. Visual ideas and notes for the commentary can be sketched on to the cards. The cards can then be arranged into the best sequence. Try, as much as you can, to think visually. Use sketches rather than written notes to help you. Remember, you are employing a visual medium so let it work to best advantage. If you find that there seems to be a large amount of talk in your developing script, critically review what you have done and perhaps consider using a sound cassette instead.

Incidentally, what is meant by the 'best sequence'? There are several ways in which you might go about answering this question, always, of course, with your content and students in mind. Desirable ways of sequencing ideas are to proceed from what students already know to what they don't know, from simple ideas to complex ones, from a whole view to a part view and from concrete ideas to abstract ideas.

The sequenced cards can then be used as the basis to write your script. The exact format of your script will depend on the complexity of the production resources at your disposal.

Recording: Before you commence recording, you must check that all participants in your project know what is expected of them, that all equipment is working satisfactorily and that the subject is well lit. A rehearsal will help you here. Video playback allows you to check your work as you go – a distinct advantage over film.

As you work, try to keep the points listed in Figure 7.6 in mind.

Editing: Your recordings will usually need to be edited by using electronic video-editing equipment. Editing is a process of selecting and joining together visual sequences in the order dictated by your script. When editing is complete, you will need to add a sound-track which is most likely to include your narration.

FIGURE 7.6
GUIDELINES FOR VIDEO RECORDING

Guidelines

- Allow the subject of your interest to provide movement. Avoid camera movement as much as possible, such as zooming in and out, panning across or tilting up and down.
- Constantly check the composition of the picture to avoid visual clutter or confusion about what is being seen.
- Remember that you are also recording sound and that this should be as clear as possible at all times.

Reviewing your programme: Once the euphoria of having completed your first recording has passed, sit down and critically review your work and make any alterations which are technically necessary and educationally desirable. When you first use the recording with students collect some information from them as well. A useful ploy is to watch students as they go through the programme. You will often be able to pick up sections that are causing difficulty or confusion.

5. TAPE–SLIDE PRESENTATIONS

Tape–slide programmes are an effective way of presenting material to students. They are also cheaper than video programmes and simpler to prepare. It is usual to devise the programme in such a way that students can work alone and at their own pace.

Visual information in the programme is presented on 35 mm slides and a commentary on a sound cassette guides and explains. In some tape-slide equipment, electronic pulses can be put on the cassette tape which will change slides automatically.

Before embarking on the production be sure to consult the earlier section in this chapter on slide preparation. Most of the principles for making an educational videocassette apply to making tape–slide programmes and you are directed back to that material for details. Briefly the main principles are as follows.

Planning: This includes writing a story-line, considering educational, technical and administrative questions and preparing a script.

Scripting: The commentary you prepare should be in simple spoken English. Avoid reading from an over-formal text and avoid indirect references such as 'these', 'they' and 'it', which may create confusion. We have found it best to use a conversational mode, imagining that you are talking to a single person. All too often tape–slide programmes are like recorded lectures. Your commentary can be made more interesting by the planned use of questions, pauses for student thinking, prerecorded sound-effects or interviews, and deliberate breaks in which short exercises or problems can be tackled. Make sure that the visual content on the screen matches the commentary. A mismatch between the visual input and the audio input will inevitably cause confusion. Part of the script from a tape–slide programme is shown in Figure 7.7.

FIGURE 7.7
PART OF A SCRIPT
FROM A TAPE-SLIDE
PROGRAMME

VISUAL	AUDIO
SLIDE 1 TITLE	THIS IS THE THIRD OF A SERIES OF TUTORIALS ON ELECTROCARDIOGRAPHY. YOU SHOULD NOW HAVE THE TITLE SLIDE SHOWING AND CORRECTLY FOCUSSED (PAUSE). LET US REVIEW SOME OF THE IMPORTANT POINTS YOU HAVE LEARNED FROM THE FIRST TWO SESSIONS.
SLIDE 2. ECG COMPLEXES	FIRST OF ALL, HOW'S YOUR TERMINOLOGY? HERE YOU SEE A LEFT-SIDED LEAD AND A RIGHT SIDED LEAD. JUST STOP THE TAPE FOR A MINUTE OR TWO AND WRITE DOWN WHAT THESE SYMBOLS MEAN THEN RESTART THE TAPE TO CONTINUE.
SLIDE 3.	HERE IS WHAT YOU SHOULD HAVE WRITTEN. "P" REPRESENTS ATRIAL DEPOLARIZATION ...

Recording: This requires much less in the way of technical expertise and facilities than video-recording. A quiet room and a good-quality tape-recorder are all that is required, though better quality can be obtained in a studio. Automatic slide-changing pulses can be added later if necessary. However, it is just as easy, and often less trouble in the long run, to include a request to change slides in the commentary. This then ensures that the programme can be used with less sophisticated equipment such as the student might have at home.

Reviewing the programme: You should make the same critical review of the presentation as suggested in the preceding section on video.

6. PRINTED MATERIALS

Books, journals, handouts and study guides carry a very large part of the instructional burden in teaching. Yet, often, surprisingly little thought is given to the design and use of these important teaching materials.

Design

Care needs to be taken in designing and preparing printed materials. Over-organization of the text does not help the reader and may actually interfere with learning. You may find it helpful to yourself and to your students to standardize on layouts and perhaps to institute a system of coloured papers for different kinds of material (eg white for lecture notes, green for bibliographies, yellow for exercises). The basic principles for layout and design of printed materials are outlined in Figure 7.8.

The variety of fonts available for personal computers and electric typewriters also makes it necessary to select with care. Have a look at the typographical layouts in better-quality newspapers and journals for ideas that you can put into practice.

Using printed material

Handouts can serve a number of useful purposes in your teaching, but this medium is frequently misused because the material is often simply distributed to students and then quickly forgotten.

Handouts can be used by students as a note-taking guide to a lecture. Supplementary information, or perhaps a copy of a paper you think is important, can also be given in a handout.

FIGURE 7.8

GUIDELINES FOR THE LAYOUT AND DESIGN OF PRINTED MATERIAL

Guidelines

Learning from printed materials can be enhanced by incorporating the folowing:

- An introduction to relate the new material to the past experience of the student.
- A summary of the major ideas or arguments presented.
- The use of major and minor headings.
- Space between paragraphs and sections to relieve the impact of too much print.
- Simplicity in expression.
- Appropriately labelled illustrations, tables and graphs (a series of diagrams building up to a complete concept may be more helpful than one detailed diagram).
- Questions and exercises within the text to stimulate thinking.

How you use the handout in your teaching is a crucial matter. We recommend that your students' attention be directed to the handout by discussing a particular definition, reading through a brief list of points with students, or getting them to fill in some part of it with additional information. If your students have to use the handout in the teaching session, it is likely that they will remember it and not simply file it away to be forgotten.

Prescribed reading

Prescribed reading of textbooks and journals is another matter that warrants your careful attention. Some teachers swamp their students with lists of books and articles to be read and give little thought to how they might manage the task. If you want the students to undertake some reading, then consider the following points:

★ What are students expected to achieve by undertaking the reading? (Make this purpose clearly known to the students.)

- How will the reading be followed up in subsequent teaching?
- Will the recommended reading be readily available in libraries or through bookshops?
- How can the reading be usefully organized? (Arrange the material in a logical fashion, indicate why an item has been listed and what is especially important about it.)

NEW TECHNOLOGIES

The microelectronics revolution has yet to make a major impact on higher education but it must inevitably occur. How it will do so is hard to predict and it is not within the scope of this book to consider the matter in detail. The growing number of households with sophisticated video equipment and computers will dramatically change the availability of information and educational materials at present restricted by limited access to libraries and audiovisual resource centres.

Anything written about computers will inevitably be out of date by the time it is published. However, in the educational arena it is not the technology that will be a critical factor but our ability to use and adapt it to our defined educational purposes. Computers have been used quite extensively in higher education for some years, particularly for computer-aided instruction, computer-based simulation, problem-solving exercises of varying complexities and computerized self-assessment programmes. Despite many pilot projects, such applications are not widely available, often being dependent on the presence or absence of an enthusiastic staff member. If you are such an enthusiast you probably know more about the subject than we do! If you are not, but see potential for the use of a computer in your teaching, then you should seek the advice of your own computing centre.

Perhaps one of the more predictable uses of the ubiquitous silicon chip is in the area of information storage. It has been estimated that an average book can be reduced to about two million 'bits' of information, a storage capacity well within that of present microcomputer discs. Optical holograms, produced by laser-beams, hold the promise of a desk-top system having a capacity of one million million bits, enough to accommodate a good-sized university library.

A similar revolution is upon us in the video world. The advanced capacities for speedy and accurate location of information on a videodisc provide the opportunity for producing interactive educational material previously limited to computers. It does not require too much imagination to think up several ways in which this facility could be of value and two of these have already been described. The essential problem to us as teachers is to know enough about these new technologies to allow us to utilize them and select those which have real value in helping us achieve our aims. We must not be seduced by the novelty nor must we let the opportunities they present pass us by.

EVALUATING TEACHING MATERIALS

Like all aspects of teaching, the materials you produce, or intend to purchase, should be carefully evaluated. Forgive us for reminding you again that the primary questions for audio and visual materials will always be 'Are they audible?' and 'Are they visible?'

A more detailed checklist of questions you should think through is provided in Figure 7.9.

FIGURE 7.9 CHECKLIST FOR EVALUATING TEACHING MATERIAL (AFTER ROE AND MCDONALD)

Relevance of the material

- Why is it used?
- How does it relate to the course unit and other materials?

Content

- Is it factually correct?
- Is it balanced?
- Is it current?
- Does it make the right assumptions about students' prior knowledge?
- Is it presented at a suitable level?

Structure

- Is it logical?
- Is it subdivided so that its structure is obvious?
- Is it an appropriate length?

Presentation

- Is the language clear?
- Are tables and illustrations used to best effect?
- Is the layout effective?
- Is it presented in an interesting fashion?
- If it is designed for independent study, can students use it without assistance?

GUIDED READING

For a comprehensive guide to the wide range of teaching aids and their preparation, you will find considerable value in J E Kemp's *Planning and Producing Audio Visual Materials* (4th Edn), Harper & Row, New York, 1980. This book also provides a helpful theoretical and research base to the educational aspects of using teaching aids.

Designing Instructional Text (2nd Edn) by J Hartley, Kogan Page, London, 1985, is highly recommended for preparing text-based materials (books, manuals, handouts, computer-generated or stored text). We used Hartely when preparing this book which may or may not be a recommendation!

Informed Professional Judgement: A Guide to Evaluation in Post-Secondary Education by E Roe and R McDonald, University of Queensland Press, Brisbane, 1983.

Chapter 8 Helping Students Learn

INTRODUCTION

The focus of this book so far has been on improving and broadening the range of teaching skills. Though we have assumed that the aim of doing so is for the ultimate benefit of the students, our emphasis has been on the personal development of the teacher. In this chapter we will introduce you to ideas which are not as widely represented in the teaching literature as those in other sections of the book. Nevertheless, we believe that they have provided valuable new insights to us and to many of our colleagues. Thus, this chapter may appear to be more theoretical than previous ones but we include it without reservation because of the fundamental challenge it provides to the more traditional views of teaching.

Teachers are generally primarily interested in **what** students learn. Over the last few years a considerable body of evidence has accumulated which suggests that we need to become much more concerned with **how** our students learn. We need to appreciate that some of our students are having difficulties with their studies arising not just from lack of application or psychosocial problems, but from specific problems with the way they study and learn. We must also appreciate that some of these problems are directly attributable to the way we teach, organize courses and conduct assessments.

HOW STUDENTS LEARN

It seems that all students (and teachers) have distinctive *approaches to learning* which are influenced by many factors, as shown in Figure 8.1.

One of these factors is dependent on personality traits and is sometimes referred to as the preferred **learning style**. Other influences can be grouped under characteristics of the teaching and characteristics of the department organizing the course. In

FIGURE 8·1

A MODEL OF STUDENT LEARNING

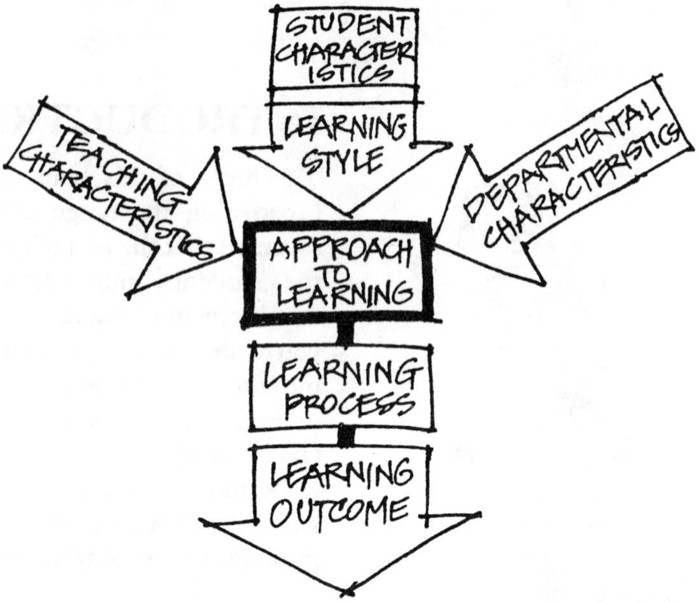

general, teaching and departmental influences seem to be more important than learning style in determining the students' approach to learning. The approach adopted subsequently determines the **learning process** or study method used by the student and this, in turn, affects the quality of the **learning outcome.**

Students can be observed to use one of three broad approaches to learning, commonly called surface, deep and strategic.

Students adopting a **surface approach** are predominantly motivated by a concern to complete the course or by a fear of failure. They intend to fulfil the assessment requirements of the course by memorizing factual material. The process they use to achieve this is rote learning. The outcome is, at best, a knowledge of factual information and a superficial level of understanding.

In contrast, students adopting a **deep approach** are motivated by an interest in the subject matter and/or by its vocational relevance. Their intention is to reach an understanding of the material. The process of achieving this varies between individual students and between students in different academic disciplines. The **operation learner** relies on a logical step-by-step approach with a cautious acceptance of generalizations only when based on evidence. There is an attention to factual and procedural detail which may include rote learning. This process is most prevalent in science departments. On the other hand, the **comprehension learner** uses a process in which the initial concern is for the broad outlines of ideas and their interconnections with previous knowledge. Such students make use of analogies and attempt to give the material personal meaning. This process is more evident in arts and social science departments. However, the most effective process is that used by the so-called **versatile learner** in whom the outcome is a deep level of understanding based on a knowledge of broad principles supported by a sound factual basis. Versatile learning does not preclude the use of rote learning when the need arises, as it frequently does in science-based courses, but the students do so with a totally different intent from those using the surface approach.

Students demonstrating the **strategic approach** may be seen to use processes similar to both the deep and surface learner. The fundamental difference lies in their motivation and intention. Such students are motivated by the need to achieve high marks and to compete with others. The outcome is a variable level of understanding which depends on what is required by the course and, particularly, the assessments.

The attributes we would hope for in a university or college student are very much those embodied in the deep approach. Disturbingly, the little evidence we have suggests that these attributes may not always be encouraged by teachers or achieved by students. Indeed there is some reason to believe that many of our teaching methods, curriculum structures and, particularly, our examining methods may be actively inhibiting the use of the deep approach and supporting the use of surface and strategic approaches.

LEARNING MORE EFFECTIVELY

The concepts outlined above are not only supported by a substantial body of evidence, but also match the impressions

we have developed over many years of teaching students. Nevertheless, we feel less comfortable proffering practical advice in the way we have done in previous chapters. This arises not only from the fact that we have only limited personal experience in applying these new concepts but also that very few other people have either! Even more importantly, there is only a limited amount of research demonstrating that changing students' approaches to learning can promote more effective learning outcomes. However, we believe there is enough evidence to offer some general points of advice.

Improving the learning environment

This must be considered at various levels. At the broadest level is the educational philosophy underlying the whole curriculum. There may be little you can do about this, but it might be as well to be aware that there is some evidence from the field of medical education that students from traditional medical schools seem to adopt the surface and strategic approaches to a greater degree than students from schools offering a problem-based curriculum. The curricula of the former tend to be highly lecture-oriented and heavy use is frequently made of objective-type (MCQ) tests. On the other hand, the problem-based schools utilize small group techniques and self-directed learning with assessments being more informal or based on tests of problem-solving ability. You may be able to gauge where the educational philosophy of your own discipline or curriculum fits and predict the likely effect it has on your students' approach to learning.

At another level, and one where you might be able to exert some influence, is the structuring of the curriculum. You should be aware that the fragmentation of the curriculum into a large number of courses or course components taught by different teachers may be counter-productive to the development of deep approaches. The time available to each is limited and so the opportunities for students to come to grips with the deeper implications and perspectives of subject matter are similarly restricted.

As most teachers reading this book will be working in a conventional institution, it would seem to be important to introduce measures into courses which might encourage the use of the deep approach. Some of these measures are listed below:

- Ensure that the course objectives specify more than just facts and technical skills by giving suitable emphasis to higher-level intellectual skills, such as problem-solving and critical thinking, and to the exploration and development of appropriate attitudes.
- Introduce teaching activities which require students to demonstrate a deep understanding of the subject matter or relevant problems. Do not allow students to 'get away' with only reproducing factual information.
- Reduce the time allocated to didactic teaching to allow more time for group-based teaching and self-directed learning.
- Decrease the amount of factual material that has to be memorized. Both pressure of time and overloading with content are known to encourage the surface approach even in those intending to use the deep approach. These problems are prevalent in many science-based courses.
- Spend more contact time in helping students to understand and use basic principles. Get into the habit of expecting students to explain answers to questions. The frequent use of the word 'why' will quickly establish if the answer is based on memorization or on an understanding of an underlying principle.
- **Most importantly,** review the assessment procedures. This is a critical task. If the assessment, course content and methods do not match the course objectives, then one could be the world's greatest teacher and make little impact on the students' learning. For example, an over-reliance on multiple-choice tests will almost certainly encourage the use of surface strategies. If you aim to have students understand the subject, then you must introduce forms of assessment which require them to demonstrate this understanding. This may mean the re-introduction of essays, project work, critical analysis of problems and so on. Students should be fully informed about the content and methods, with examples provided.

Modifying teaching styles

Teachers need to be aware that they have teaching style preferences for the same reasons that students have preferred learning styles. It is unlikely that these preferences will match those of all students. The importance of this issue is uncertain but there is experimental evidence that a match of teaching and learning styles produces more effective learning.

It seems reasonable to suggest that teachers should develop skills which are likely to enhance the learning of all students, not just those with whom they may have a natural affinity. In the lecture situation, for instance, teachers who prefer to present material in a very logical and structured way may be popular with students with a preference for operation learning, but less so with students with a bent towards comprehension learning. The latter may be particularly assisted by the inclusion of an overview at the beginning of the lecture and analogies to place the material in a suitable context. In small groups, on the other hand, operation learners may be relatively uncomfortable with unstructured teaching.

As we know that operation learners are more prevalent in science-based disciplines, this may explain why lectures seem to dominate their teaching activities, often it seems with the collusion of both students and their teachers! Nevertheless, this may not be the ideal way of teaching important aspects of such courses. It is important that you appreciate this and are prepared to broaden your approach in the best interest of the overall development and learning of your students.

Improving study skills

There seems little doubt that good study skills contribute to academic success, though in themselves they are not a guarantee of success. Skills must be tied to a positive attitude and motivation to the subject. Being well-organized and efficient in the use of time and resources is important. However, it is clear that there is no correct way to study, which may be why the use of study manuals and courses in study methods have not been very successful. Special counsellors may be valuable for students with severe problems but there is a growing recognition that subject teachers should become more interested in helping students individually within the context of their own courses. An interview should make it possible to identify the problem area:

- **Social factors:** too much time involved in extracurricular activities; social motivation higher than academic.
- **Psychological factors:** undue anxiety; interpersonal problems.
- **Specific study skill problems:** poor scheduling of time; lack of study plan; inappropriate study environment; inadequate preparation for examinations; poor examination techniques.

For further information and help with study skill counselling we refer you to the book by Gibbs which is recent enough to take into account some of the new understanding about student learning that we described earlier in the chapter.

GUIDED READING

For a review of the research on which the ideas presented in this chapter have been based, we refer you to the following:

'Learning styles and approaches: implications for medical education' by D I Newble and N J Entwistle, *Medical Education*, **20**: 162-75, 1986.

Improving Learning: New Perspectives Ramsden, P (Ed) Kogan Page, London (1988).

There are many books on study skills. One that we find provides a balance of theory and practice is G Gibbs' *Teaching Students to Learn: A Student-Centred Approach*, The Open University Press, Milton Keynes, UK, 1981.

Another paperback, containing a lot of detailed advice on both how to study and how to perform various academic tasks is *A Guide to Learning Independently* by L Marshall and F Rowland, Longman Cheshire, Melbourne, Australia, 1981. Though written for students it is of equal value to teachers.

Index